THE COMING STORM

1812

David Griggs

Copyright Page

Preface

In the annals of history, certain periods stand out as tumultuous crossroads, where the fate of nations hangs in the balance. The War of 1812 was one such epoch, a tempest that swept across North America, its winds of change reshaping loyalties and destinies alike. Born from the smoldering embers of the War of Independence, it was a conflict that pitted brother against brother, nation against nation, and freedom against empire.

In the shadow of this brewing storm, amidst the chaos of clashing allegiances and fervent patriotism, there were those who sought no part in the political machinations that drove the land towards conflict. Among them were Nathan Douglas, a weathered American sailor, and Mary Johnson, a steadfast loyalist of the United Empire. Two souls bound by circumstance rather than conviction, their paths converged amidst the tumult of war, forging an unlikely alliance in the crucible of adversity.

As the drums of war thundered ever closer, Nathan and Mary found themselves thrust into a precarious dance of survival, where every step could lead to salvation or ruin. United by the common goal of navigating the treacherous waters of uncertainty, they must confront not only the external threats that assail them but also the inner demons that threaten to tear apart the fragile fabric of their alliance.

Amidst the smoke and thunder of cannon fire, "The Coming Storm" unfolds—a tale of courage and resilience, of love and loyalty, set against the backdrop of a nation torn asunder. Within these pages, readers will embark on a journey fraught with peril and intrigue, where the bonds of friendship are tested, and the true cost of freedom is laid bare.

Brace yourself for the tempest that lies ahead, for within these pages, the echoes of history resound, and the winds of change blow fiercely. For Nathan and Mary, the storm is but the beginning of their odyssey, a journey that will forever alter the course of their lives and the destiny of a nation.

Chapter 1

The gentle breezes blew softly across the water's surface, as the sun's rays kissed the waves with their glistening warmth. The icy grip of winter was long forgotten as the leaves of the trees, in rhythmic motion, seemed to welcome the sailors back. It had been an unusually harsh winter. The frozen waters had refused passage to all ships seeking to make their way along the southern shores of Lake Ontario. Those who depended upon the waters for their supplies had to find other ways to keep their storehouses full.

Peggy, a schooner owned by the merchant Matthew McNair, had sat in dry dock awaiting the return of the warmer weather. Peggy was a sister ship to Diana, built in Oswego, for sailing the waters of Lake Ontario. Since bringing supplies by land was labor intensive, the merchants of the settlements depended on the waterways for their provisions. As winter gave way to spring, merchants and settlers alike were eager for the first signs of the new shipping season.

The captain of the Peggy, along with the first mate, had not been idle during the winter months. Peggy needed the usual overhaul to prepare for the new shipping season. It was necessary to check the masts and sails. The ship's bowels were prepared for the crew. Ample storage space had to be found for the merchant's wares. Anything that would not bring profit for the owner was to be removed. The more cargo that Peggy could carry, the more money was to be made for McNair and his business partners.

Though the ship had been in dry dock, the owners were not idle. They had sent their agents to the various ports to secure orders for the coming shipping season. These agents traveled mostly along the routes that the ship would take. Since the War of Independence, McNair preferred to travel along the southern shores of Lake Ontario. Though the ports of Kingston and York held prospect for greater business, most American ship owners decided not to antagonize the British by sailing into their harbors. Peace accords were always tenuous at best and not to be tested. There was still much money to be made in the burgeoning growth of the many merchants and settlers along the southern shores.

Nathan Douglas had been employed as First Mate on the Peggy for the last year and a half. Originally from Vermont, he loved the water and the freedom that it brought. Being the eldest son of Samuel and Rebecca, he grew up on the waters of Lake Champlain, as Burlington quickly became a major trade center. Near Lower Canada and especially Montreal, trade flowed freely between the two countries. The War of Independence did little to dampen the spirit of the entrepreneurs.

Nathan, as a young child, would watch as the ships sailed into the wharves of Burlington. He loved the tall masts and expansive sails, often waiting by the shores of Lake Champlain, to see the ships come and go. His parents knew he would not be a landlubber, someone unfamiliar with the waters. The waters called to him, and he answered the call. Leaving home at nineteen, he found employment on the Peggy at Oswego. His skill quickly brought praise from the captain, trusting him with the safety and security of the ship, as well as giving oversight to the ship's crew. At age twenty-one, Nathan became an integral part of the success of the Peggy.

Like most sailors, Nathan couldn't wait for the new shipping season to begin. He had been busy with the captain, hiring those needed for the Peggy. There were sailors from the previous years; others looking for work and those who had never dipped their toe in any waters. He would need to rely on those seasoned sailors to carry the workload as he did "on-the-job" training with the novices.

His favorite was the cook, Thomas. He had been with the Peggy since the day it was commissioned and ruled the galley as his own domain. The new recruits quickly found out that though he may not be the captain, he was the real boss of the ship.

The Peggy set sail from Oswego in mid-May. Their course took them along the southern coastline of Lake Ontario, arriving in Rochester. Rochester had become a bustling community, especially after the War of Independence. As the Peggy drew near to the port of Rochester, other ships were also lined up along the docks, waiting for their cargo to be loaded. Yet the agents of McNair had expected their arrival so that when the Peggy arrived, the cargo was ready to load.

Shipping is not a gentleman's business and etiquette is not to be found by anyone, sailor, or dock hand. The goal was not to make friends or be cordial. The cargo was to be loaded quickly and efficiently. Time down is money and money makes the business profitable. The quicker the cargo could be loaded, the sooner they could set sail.

Nathan had a gift for getting the most out of those who worked on the Peggy. He was not there to be their friend. They were not there to be idle. Anyone found not carrying his weight was reprimanded once and then told to find other employment. They knew what was expected of them and most performed as required. After all, winter was a long time to not have employment. But Nathan was an excellent judge of character and hired those that he was sure would make it.

Nathan and the captain had already spent the winter planning how the cargo was to be loaded. There is an order necessary to maximize the space with as much cargo as possible. He was not about to leave any cargo on the docks. With a quick eye to detail, he directed his crew in what to bring on board and where to place it. In single file and each carrying his weight, the cargo was quickly loaded.

Finally, the last barrel was secured, and the dock space cleared. The captain gave the order, and the Peggy pushed away from the docks to begin the journey south.

Chapter 2

Nathan loved the open waters. There was something about being unencumbered by any of the cares of life. Lake Ontario, in the Huron language, meant "Lake of Shining Waters" and today it lived up to its name. As the sails filled with the north-east winds, the Peggy moved gracefully across the waters at a speed of five knots.

McNair's agents had met during the winter months with Mary Johnson, the overseer of the estate of Robert Hamilton. Hamilton had been a wealthy merchant, having lived at Queenston in Upper Canada. He had made his fortune as a merchant, whiskey maker, tanner and financier to the many inhabitants who now dotted the landscape of the Niagara Region. He had grown wealthy through trade and commerce, but especially as a major lender to the many landowners, Hamilton benefited most when they defaulted on their debts. Through their misfortune, he had gained vast land holdings. Some saw this as greed. He saw it as being a shrewd business owner.

The cargo, now loaded onto the Peggy, was destined for the Hamilton estate in Queenston. The scheduled time of arrival in Queenston was about thirty hours after leaving Rochester.

Nathan had assigned the various tasks necessary for the crew to keep the ship running smoothly and efficiently. When they were not on duty, the most frequented place was the galley. Thomas kept their plates full and the rum flowing even more.

This day started off like any other day. Nothing unusual and nothing planned beyond the normal. As the ship sailed gracefully across the glistening waters, the captain stood with an eyeglass in hand, observing the movement of a larger vessel moving in their direction. It was not odd to see other ships going back and forth across the waters. Lake Ontario joined the St. Lawrence River with the Niagara River and points even further south.

Yet the larger vessel seemed to be on an intercept course for the Peggy. As it drew closer and became more focused in the eyeglass, the captain let out a curse and called the first mate to his side.

"Seems like we are going to have company," the captain mused.

"Can you tell who it is?"

"They're flying the British flag, with the colors of the Royal George. Get the crew ready," he ordered.

The Royal George was a 22-gun sloop, built at the shipyards in Kingston. She carried a crew of 200 sailors and was the largest warship on Lake Ontario. She was not to be trifled with, nor was her captain, Hugh Earl.

He had earned a reputation as a no-nonsense leader, able and willing to impose British supremacy upon the waterways.

The captain of the Peggy had known of the harassing nature of the British navy. Though he himself had never been boarded, he had known of others who had. Each one told of his unpleasant experience. The British were intent on disrupting any commerce by the Americans. But it was the hated policy of impressment that struck fear into the hearts of captains. Armed gangs would board merchant ships and forcibly press men into service in the British navy. Some captains spoke of their own ships being left without sufficient manpower for their own journeys.

The Royal George and the Peggy were on an unmistakable collision course on the "Lake of Shining Waters". The Royal George approached, positioning its guns to face the Peggy. There would be no escape if the meeting turned violent.

"Heave to and prepare to be boarded."

"What do you want, and why do you wish to board us? We are flying the flag of the United States of America and are under its protection."

"And are they here to protect you?" shouted back Hugh Earl. "If you do not heave to and prepare to be boarded, there will be nothing left for them to protect."

The captain of the Peggy waited but for a moment before uttering the order, "Prepare to receive the men of the Royal George."

Grappling hooks and lines were tossed, securing the Royal George to the Peggy. Nathan could only watch as armed sailors boarded. There was nothing he could do. There was nothing anyone on the Peggy could do. The British marines leaped from their own gunwale to the Peggy's deck.

"Where is your captain?" shouted the officer in charge.

"I am here. What do you want, and what do you mean by this intrusion? I will lodge a formal complaint to the United States government for this." The captain's eyes glared fiercely.

Ignoring him, the officer commanded his marines to begin their search. The crew of the Peggy were ordered to stand fast and not hinder the search. No one could follow any of the marines into the hold of the Peggy.

The time seemed to drag as the two ships bobbed on the water's surface. The Peggy was clearly the smaller of the two vessels. Finally, the marines returned from the holds of the Peggy. Only this time, they were not alone. Thomas stood before them, hands and feet shackled.

"Why was this man not ordered to be on the deck with the others?" demanded the officer.

"Thomas is our cook and was likely in the galley preparing food," Nathan shot back.

"I'm not talking to you. Be silent or I will shackle you as well." The lieutenant approached Nathan.

Without hesitation, the captain of the Peggy intervened to protect Nathan.

"It's as the first mate said. Thomas was in the galley preparing our meals. He's an American citizen."

"No matter. We need a cook, and he is coming with us. Do you wish to argue the point any further?"

The captain's eyes met those of the armed marines. He had no words. There was no recourse for him or anyone else. The argument had ended. Thomas was going with the Royal George.

The British sailors, with Thomas in tow, boarded the Royal George. The British released the grappling hooks and lines, pushing away to start their journey back on Lake Ontario.

The crew of the Peggy watched as the Royal George grew more distant. Finally, the captain shouted, "Quit standing around and get to work. Find me another cook."

Chapter 3

As the Peggy continued its journey towards Niagara, Nathan thought about what had just happened. He had heard the stories of the injustices by the British towards his parents and grandparents. This is the first time that he had experienced these himself.

Nathan's parents, Samuel, and Rebecca Douglas had moved to Burlington from Albany following the War of Independence. Their parents had emigrated from Scotland to begin a new life in Albany, following the end of the French and Indian wars. Thousands of British merchants and soldiers also made their way to Albany, each hoping to prosper in the new world. For a time, the Douglas family did just that. But not all was well in Albany.

The British believed they had lost the French war in 1755 in upper New York because there were not enough billets for their soldiers during the winter months. They were determined not to make the same mistake. The British governor, Loudoun, ordered the council of Albany to build more barracks for his troops. The Albanians agreed to provide some funds and land towards this, but they would not assume the full costs. Loudon made a decision that inflamed the people of Albany. If there were not enough barracks to house the British troops, they would be "Quartered" in the homes of the Albanians. Each home was to provide beds and spaces for the troops.

The Douglas' were not opposed to this order at first. The 42nd Royal Highlanders, known as the Black Watch, had settled among the people of Albany. They were Scotsmen, their kin, and they were glad to house some of them.

Most of the 42nd were respectful and courteous to their hosts, but not all. Some were brutish, demanding more than the Douglas' were required to give. They ate their food. They broke furniture in their drunken states. Their behavior became intolerable.

A ground swell of complaints arose among the Albanians. No longer was it "us" but "we and them". The complaints boiled over into mob riots and even violence against the soldiers. Nathan's grandparents could not and did not stay away from the fracas. They had embraced Albany as their home, seeking to build a life for themselves and their family. Even though they were loyal to King George, they were now being treated as colonialists and not as British subjects.

This change in mindset set forth policies by the British government that would change the course of history for the people of Albany and for the

Douglas'. The people longed for equal citizenship. The British desired only subjugation.

Nathan had heard these stories many times from his father. "We are Americans. As much as your grandparents loved Scotland, Albany became their home, and they fought to give you your freedom from the oppressors."

Samuel's father had joined the Patriots in their ultimate quest for independence. When the declaration of independence was drafted, he embraced it wholeheartedly. He had experienced the tyranny firsthand, with troops quartered in his house. It was time to be free of British rule.

"The history of the present King of Great Britain is a history of repeated injuries and usurpations, all having in direct object the establishment of an absolute tyranny over these states … He has combined with others to subject us to a jurisdiction foreign to our constitution, and unacknowledged by our laws, giving his assent to their acts of pretended legislation: for quartering large bodies of armed troops among us."

Following the war, Nathan's grandfather joined "the Albany Committee of Safety", a group determined to root out and remove those who were still loyal to the British crown. They interviewed many suspected Loyalists, finding only a small number they would consider true loyalists. What they found were many who were simply caught in the middle of a conflict that they wanted no part of. Many citizens had sought to remain neutral so that, regardless of who won, they could still keep their place in Albanian society.

The Albany Committee of Safety saw it differently. They fined, imprisoned, and banished any who spoke against the American cause. Nathan's grandfather had accompanied the sheriff, rounding up the "disaffected" and bringing them before the committee. Lands were confiscated and perceived traitors to the cause were forced to leave or risk imprisonment.

The Douglas family benefited from this purging of those not loyal to the cause. They were rewarded with confiscated properties and possessions. This Scotsman, once loyal to the British crown, now became a man of wealth and position among the people of Albany.

After Nathan's grandparents died, Samuel was left with a considerable estate. But with that estate also came many unresolved conflicts. When the war was over, petty jealousies arose among those who had belonged to the Committee of Safety. Friends now became distant, even antagonistic towards one other. Life for Samuel and Rebecca became increasingly difficult as they faced this growing tide of opposition.

The time came for them to leave. Settling their accounts and selling their properties, they left for the regions of Burlington, Vermont, a bustling, growing center of commerce in the northeast. Here they would begin a new life. Here Nathan would be born, the eldest son and future sailor on the waters of Lake Ontario.

As the Royal George sailed off onto the horizon, Nathan simply nodded, the waves of the lake echoing the tumult of his thoughts. The journey across the waters of Lake Ontario seemed to bridge the gap between his past and present, carrying him back to the roots of his family's struggle against tyranny.

Memories of his grandparents' tumultuous departure from Albany still echoed in his mind, their flight from conflict leaving behind a legacy of unresolved grievances. Nathan couldn't help but feel a kinship with their journey, a shared defiance against the injustices that had torn their lives apart.

With each gust of wind that filled the sails of the Peggy, Nathan felt the weight of his family's history pressing down on him, a reminder of the sacrifices that had
brought him to this moment. And as he gazed out across the vast expanse of the lake, he realized that his destiny lay not only in the waters before him but also in the legacy of courage and resilience that had been passed down through generations.

In that fleeting moment, as the ship disappeared into the distance, Nathan found himself at peace with the choices that had brought him here. His grandfather's decision to take up arms against the British was not just a rebellion against oppression, but a testament to the indomitable spirit of those who refused to be silenced in the face of injustice.

With a newfound sense of purpose, Nathan turned his gaze towards the horizon, the promise of adventure and discovery beckoning him forward. For in the waters of Lake Ontario, he saw not only the legacy of his ancestors but also the boundless potential of his own future, waiting to be explored with each passing wave.

Chapter 4

The Peggy sailed effortlessly across the waters of Lake Ontario. They had encountered no more ships, nor did they wish to see any. From the starboard side, Nathan could see the town of York, still in a distance. Along the port side was the rugged wilderness of the south shore of the lake. No one had yet settled into the arduous task of homesteading on these shores. The odd deer could be seen drinking from the water's edges as seagulls danced in the morning breezes above them.

Nathan felt a pang in his belly and knew that this was normally the time when Thomas would fill his plate with his favorite foods. But Thomas was now lost to them, and Nathan had found no one. True, he could simply order someone to take up the culinary tasks of the galley, but food poisoning and unhappy sailors was the last thing he needed.

As he made his way down to the galley, he heard clanging noises coming from within. Entering, he saw Bjorn effortlessly going about, making himself and a few others something to eat. Bjorn had joined them late in the shipping season. Nathan knew little about him except that he worked hard and got along with the others.

Bjorn saw Nathan coming into the galley.

"Mate, with Thomas gone, we were getting hungry. I hope it's okay that we, that I, make us something to eat," he asked sheepishly.

"We all have to eat. Do you have enough for me?" Nathan quizzed.

"Aye, Mate. Pull up a chair and Bjorn will get you a plate."

Bjorn soon brought him a plate and utensils, followed by a goulash mix slopped splat on Nathan's plate.

"What is it?" Nathan asked, unsure whether he should eat or get his own food.

"Ah, it's what my mama made when I was a boy. Eat up. You will like it," he said, with a twinkle in his eye.

Nathan brought a small portion to his lips.

"This is good," he said. "Is this all that you know how to make?"

"Nah, my mama taught me how to cook. She said, 'Bjorn, there's going to be a time when your mama's no longer around to make your meals. You must learn to cook and take care of yourself.' My mama taught me how to cook and she taught me well," he said, patting himself on his belly.

"I need a cook and you are going to be that person. Until we can make other arrangements, I want you to get the meals for the men. Okay?" he said, without really expecting an answer.

"Jah, I knew you would ask, and I like to cook." Bjorn turned away to dish out meals for others who sat patiently, or rather impatiently, for their food.

Nathan finished and, with a nod of appreciation, made his way out of the galley and back to the deck. The captain was still standing on the fore when Nathan drew near.

"I have found an excellent cook for us. That Swede, Bjorn," he offered.

The captain only glanced at him, keeping his eyes fixed on what lay ahead.

The Peggy was nearing the mouth of the Niagara River, where it emptied into the waters of Lake Ontario. These moments were always quiet moments for the captain. Along the river were two forts. Fort Niagara, on the American side, was now under American control by the Jay Treaty of 1795. As long as the captain flew the flag of the American states, he felt secure along these banks.

It was the other fort that concerned him. Fort George, on the outskirts of Newark, controlled the upper regions of the lower Niagara. He was soon to pass by this fort as he made his way towards Queenston.

The sailors continued their routines as they made their way up the Niagara River. Yet all were silent. Maybe it was the recent memories of a visit from the Royal George that made them wary. Maybe it was the unsettling of events that had reached them in Oswego and Rochester, news of a coming conflict. They knew that once passed Fort Niagara, the guns of Fort George would follow their progress. Regardless, the Jay Treaty had secured them the rights of open commerce. For the moment, they were secure in this.

Chapter 5

The bell clanged loudly as the Peggy's sails came into view. The people of Queenston were awaiting her arrival, laden with their treasures. Well, not really theirs, but belonging to the estate of Robert Hamilton. Regardless, it was not every day that they received such a welcomed gift into their community.

Queenston was a small community of about 20 cottages of various sizes. Most of the people were United Empire Loyalists who had settled into the Niagara Region of Upper Canada, following the American Revolution. It was all about perspective. These residents saw themselves as loyal subjects of King George and the British Empire. For them, the Americans had revolted against British rule. With Britain's loss, many of the settlers chose not to remain under the American flag and, petitioning the British crown, were granted property rights in Niagara. Others had fled to Niagara, after having been forced from their homes by committees, such as were found in Albany.

The Peggy drew near to the docks of Queenston, still flying the American flag. For many of these residents, it was all about commerce and trade, not politics. As such, the children and even adults stood on the banks of the Niagara River to greet the first ship of the new season into their community.

The captain stood on the starboard side as the Peggy drew near to dock. He was observing the crowds, knowing that not all would welcome their arrival into a British dock. Resentments from past injuries seldom get forgotten, especially from those who had lost family and property in the war.

Nathan went down onto the deck to supervise his men as they cast their hawsers or mooring lines to those waiting on the dock. The Peggy needed to be firmly secured before any cargo was unloaded. A bobbing ship, not properly fastened, can damage the cargo, or even bring death to any of his men. He observed as the dock hands received the lines and attached them to the bollards. Only then did Nathan give the order to connect the gang planks from the ship to the dock.

Overlooking the docks was an impressive, two-story house that seemed to tower above the other houses. The exterior was made of Greystone, having side wings and covered galleries running the full length of the house. Nestled in a clear, forested area, it exuded opulence and wealth.

The front door of the house opened. A young woman came out and made her way down the walkway towards the Peggy. She looked to be about eighteen, though probably older, but had an air of confidence, even authority, as she walked. As she neared the docks, Nathan took a step back so that he could better appreciate the scenery, not that he was now looking at the house. She had definitely caught his eye as she moved towards him - her delicate features with sky-blue eyes, a button nose and delicate lips. For a moment, he needed to catch his breath.

"I'm looking for the captain," she said.

"The captain is still on the ship, but I'm the first mate. How can I help you?" he said, with a twinkle in his eye.

She ignored his obvious flirtation.

"Is this cargo for the Hamilton estate?"

"Yes, it is," Nathan said, a bit curtly.

"I oversee the Hamilton estate and am here to see that you do your job correctly. The last thing we need is damaged crates."

"We know our job and how to handle your cargo," he said, with a slight emphasis on your cargo.

With his hand outstretched, he continued his speech.

"My name is Nathan, Nathan Douglas. What might be your name?" he asked.

She ignored the hand.

"Mary Johnson. How long will this take? I have men coming to take the cargo to the storehouses."

"A little longer if you don't quit talking and let me do my job," he said, rather sarcastically.

Nathan, tall and good looking, had this sense about him. He was a lady's man, a debonair. Any woman would consider him a catch, except maybe this one standing before him.

With a crisp order, he directed the men to unload the cargo onto the dock. His men had been around Nathan enough to know that the command was not about them doing their work, but trying to show this young lady that he was in charge.

"All for show," they whispered among themselves. The captain simply stood back, with a wry grin but still keeping a sharp eye on the growing crowd.

Mary had a copy of the purchase order that she had given to the owner's agents the previous winter. As the crates and barrels were being unloaded, she checked to make sure they were as ordered and undamaged. With each crate, the dock became fuller and busier.

Mary's hired men had now arrived, prepared to move the cargo to the storehouses. There, they would be unpacked and sorted. But for now, she supervised both aspects of the cargo, the unloading and reloading onto wagons. As each wagon was loaded, the wagon master nudged the horses to begin their trek. They had done this before and needed little coaxing from the drivers.

But even as Mary focused on the task at hand, her thoughts turned to the story of Robert Hamilton, the former owner of the estate. Once a formidable figure in the world of commerce, Hamilton had amassed a vast fortune through his shrewd business dealings and lavish entertainment. However, his wealth had ultimately proved powerless in the face of his impending sickness and death.

With his passing, the estate had fallen into the hands of his children, none of whom possessed the same acumen or connections as their father. As a result, the once-thriving empire had unraveled, a stark reminder of the fleeting nature of wealth and power in a world governed by uncertainty and change.

Mary Johnson had shown herself to be a resourceful manager. She had come to the Hamilton estate on a recommendation by Laura Secord, a friend of the family. Laura's husband, James Secord, owned a small merchant store on their property. He had sold produce to the local farmers. Mary's mother had died giving birth to Mary, and Laura took an interest in this young lady.

As Mary grew older, the managing of the home fell to her, as her father worked the land to provide for their needs. When the crops failed to yield and the finances became lean, Mary's father, George, had secured a loan from the estate of Robert Hamilton. Unable to repay the loan, the Johnson homestead was on the verge of being foreclosed and merged into the larger holdings of the
Hamilton family. Laura Secord intervened on behalf of the Johnson family. Mary would pay the debt by giving administrative oversight to the Hamilton estate and George could keep his land.

As the unloading neared completion, Mary leaned back to take it all in. The dock has been cleared efficiently and her hired men were loading the final cargo into the wagons. Her eyes sought to focus on the task at hand but kept drifting toward this cocky but good looking first mate. He had removed his shirt as he helped move the cargo. His muscles bulged in the outline of a deep tan. She tried hard not to look his way, but nature's drawings are sometimes too much, even for this young lady from Queenston.

"We need to settle accounts," she said. "Do I do this with you or your captain?"

Nathan turned to look at the captain, still standing on the starboard side of the ship. It was as if he was looking for something, or maybe someone. With only a nod, Nathan was to settle the account before they set sail. Wiping the sweat from his brow, he grabbed his shirt and draped it over his shoulders.

"Follow me to the house," she said. "And put your shirt on before you enter Mr. Hamilton's house."

Nathan fell in behind her as they walked back up the pathway that led to this huge Georgian structure. But it was not the house that captured Nathan's gaze. He couldn't help himself. She was attractive and walked with grace. He watched every step, every move she made as they entered the house. They made their way to the study, where the accounts would be settled, and they both could be on their way.

Chapter 6

Mary sat behind the lavish desk. Nathan stood before her. This was once Hamilton's library, with wall-to-wall bookshelves and a portrait painting of Robert Hamilton, looking over Mary's shoulder.

"Have you read any of these books?" Nathan asked, looking around.

"I have looked at some, but I have little time for reading. Mr. Hamilton was a lover of education, encouraging his children to read. He wanted them to have a fine education and even sent them to Scotland to study," she said.

"I guess I never had much time for reading myself," Nathan said. "I have always loved the waters and sailing. Ain't many bookshelves on schooners."

Mary continued to go over the invoices, ensuring that everything was in order. Actually, she was taking longer than she would normally. It was rather nice being with this tall, good-looking sailor from Oswego.

"Have you always lived in Oswego?" she asked.

"No, my folks live in Burlington, Vermont. That's where I grew to love the water."

"I have never been outside of this area," she said. "After my parents and grandparents came here, this became home for us."

"You've been here all your life?" he asked. "Where did your folks come from before they came here?"

Nathan saw a way to engage her in conversation, at least small talk.

"My grandparents are from Albany. They had a small farm outside of the town before the revolution. They had a few cattle and grew their own food. Dad says that they used to go into Albany and sell their produce to help pay expenses."

"Albany?" Nathan said. Then he paused. It is better to let Mary talk and see where this goes.

"My grandparents worked very hard building a home for my dad. Maybe that's where he got his love of farming. He couldn't wait to be in the fields, feel the dirt between his fingers, watch the crops grow from seedling to harvest. He's still the same today." She had a far off look in her eyes as she told this story. "The war changed all that for us."

"I don't know why I am telling you all this," she said. "You need to return to your ship."

"We aren't leaving for a while and I have some time to spare," almost begging her to continue.

"We weren't really political people. Dad said that by the time they milked the cows in the early morning and came in from the fields late at night, there wasn't time for much else. They just wanted to be left alone, but the war wouldn't leave them alone. They had heard, after the British troops had left, some people from Albany made up a committee, called something like a Safety Committee."

She looked down at her invoices once more, as if she was talking into space, as if no one was listening. But by this time, Nathan was all ears.

"My grandparents came from Aberdeen, Scotland and emigrated to raise their family in the new world. There were other Scottish families in Albany. When time allowed, they would all get together to talk about the old world, the new world and what was happening in Albany."

"My grandfather had a good friend, a Douglas. Didn't you say that your last name was Douglas? Oh, but then you are from Burlington, not Albany. This Douglas kept wanting my grandfather to join him in the fight against the British. It was always about fighting the British, as if he wasn't British himself. They just wanted to be left alone, but he wouldn't leave them alone. 'Either you are for them, or you are for us', he kept saying." Her voice trailed off in the silence.

"My dad and grandparents were home one night when there was a knock on the door. It was the Kemp boy, telling us we needed to leave right away. 'The Committee is coming to arrest all the men and put them in jail.' They left through the back and into the woods, hoping that no one saw them leave. The Kemp boy stood by the lane, and they asked him if he had seen the Johnsons. He told them they had left hours ago, towards Schenectady, he thought. My grandfather said that the man leading the group was his friend, Mr. Douglas."

Mary paused as a tear crept down her cheek. She pulled her handkerchief from her sleeve and dabbed at her eyes.

"Understand these people in Queenston. They are good people, but they lost everything in that war, family and friends and possessions. My grandparents left with only what they could carry and had to start over. When they see the American flag flying over your ship, it reminds them of their loss."

Mary was satisfied that the invoices were correct and was about to make payment for the cargo when there was a knock at the door. The second mate stood in the doorway.

"Sorry, miss, but the captain says that we must go now. Grab your things, Nathan, and let's go. The ship sails in five minutes."

Mary made payment and Nathan, eyes locked on hers and with a nod, turned. He was quickly out the door, down the walkway, and onto the ship.

A crowd had gathered on the shores of the Niagara River, but not as welcoming as before. There was a rising sense of danger in their midst as voices stirred the crowd into a frenzy.

The Peggy's planks were secured. The mooring lines loosened as she set sail. For now, they were safe, or so it seemed.

As she sailed down the Niagara River towards Lake Ontario, the skies darkened with a coming storm, but not every storm cloud is of nature. There was a political storm brewing that even Nathan would be powerless to escape.

Chapter 7

Napoleon had been waging war against continental Europe and Great Britain for two decades. His Berlin Decree had ordered a blockade against all shipping by Britain. All European ports under French control were to be closed to British ships. All neutral and French ships were to be seized if they entered a British port.

Britain countered by ordering that all neutral ships get a license before they sail to Europe. The Americans sought to remain neutral in this conflict, but trade was important for a thriving economy. British ships searched American "neutral" ships for contraband goods and deserters from the Royal Navy. Deserters often left the British navy to find jobs on American ships. As seen by the Royal George's boarding of the Peggy, they were willing to "impress" or seize even American sailors if they so desired.

A major naval incident had occurred earlier at Chesapeake Bay while the British were seeking French ships. Several British sailors had deserted to the American 38-gun frigate Chesapeake. When orders to "heave to" by the British 50-gun Leopard, the Chesapeake refused. The Leopard opened fire, resulting in the deaths of three sailors on the Chesapeake and injuring eighteen.

More moderate politicians, on both sides, sought to find resolution to the maritime conflicts between the American and British navies. The merchants of New England and New York pressed for peaceable solutions, but there were others who desired neither peace nor resolution, except through military intervention. The "War Hawks", from the south and west of the United States, were pressing Madison's government for an invasion of Canada. Britain must be completely removed from North America.

Dearborn, an American general, had written that Canada, in the event of war, would be easy pickings and that an invasion by an American army would be welcomed by the Canadians. Many Americans had settled in Canada since the War of Independence, drawn by free land and low taxes. Dearborn believed that these would embrace their American brethren.

As the Peggy sailed its way up the coastline of Lake Ontario, bound for its chief port at Oswego, the specter of war loomed large on the horizon. The recent declaration of war by President James
Madison had set the stage for a new chapter of conflict between the United States and Great Britain.

The War Hawks, emboldened by former President Jefferson's rhetoric, had eagerly supported the cause of war, believing that conquering Canada would be a "mere matter of marching." For them, this war represented a

Second War of Independence, a chance to rid North America of British tyranny once and for all.

With Congress approving Madison's request for war on June 4 and the Senate following suit on June 17, the die had been cast. On June 18, 1812, James Madison, the President of the United States of America had wielded his pen to commit his country to a second conflict with Great Britain.

However, as the Peggy navigated the waters of Lake Ontario, it became increasingly apparent that the British navy still held sway over the lakes. With the
declaration of war, no commercial ship flying an American flag was safe from the threat of interception and seizure by British forces.

As tensions simmered and the possibility of armed conflict grew ever closer, the crew of the Peggy braced themselves for the uncertain journey ahead, knowing that they sailed into waters fraught with danger and uncertainty.

Peggy's owner, McNair, had been in negotiations with the American navy about purchasing the Diana, now at anchor in Sacket's Harbor. But Peggy was only a merchant ship, not able to be fitted for military use. No longer able to sail the waters of Lake Ontario, the sailors were released and Nathan Douglas, first mate, was now out of work.

Now what? Where does he go? These questions he thought about as he wondered what his future would look like. He could return to Burlington and help his father in business, but his love was for the water, not a merchant's store. He could travel to Sacket's Harbor and join the American navy, but he had no desire to be a sailor on an American warship.

There was one place that drew him back. He had met this woman on his last journey to Queenston, tall with blue eyes, a button nose, and delicate lips. Packing only what he could carry, he set out. Only this time, it would not be by water but across land.

Chapter 8

The early days of the war were not quite what the American generals had hoped. Though the British troops were vastly outnumbered by the American forces, what they had was a seasoned and gifted leader by the name of General Brock. Brock had expected the coming conflict and for the previous five months was busy fortifying the Canadian defenses, mobilizing and training the local militias, and creating alliances with the native tribes.

General Hull's invasion of Canada in August proved to be ineffective and did nothing but give the Canadians more resolve to defend their territory. General Isaac Brock, with the British regulars, militia and First Nations, duped Hull into surrendering Fort Detroit with minor loss of life. Hull's Ohio militia was escorted south. His other militias had gone home to their farms and the American regulars were being sent as prisoners to Quebec City.

A letter, written by Peter Porter, quarter-master general, to the governor of New York outlined the surrender of Fort Detroit and how it had fortified the resolve of the Canadians to withstand any invasion by the American troops. Before the American prisoners were sent to Quebec City, they were garrisoned at Fort George. Porter witnessed the resolve of General Brock to deal harshly with any British subject who would join the Americans in the fight against Canada. "Many men were shot at Fort George in view of our troops (American). They are supposed to be the unfortunate fellows who joined General Hull in Canada and were surrendered at Detroit, and for who protections, provision should have been made in the capitulation at the expense of the life of every man in the garrison."

As Nathan neared Lewiston after completing his cross-country trek, his thoughts turned to the recent developments regarding allegiance to King George IV in Canada. The British had issued a stern order, mandating that all residents of Canada must pledge loyalty to the King. Those unwilling to comply faced the harsh penalties of forced removal or imprisonment. The reach of these directives extended beyond the borders of Canada, casting a shadow over the Safety Committees of Albany, which found themselves uncomfortably close to the frontier.

Amidst these tumultuous times, Nathan's focus remained fixed on his own personal journey. Arriving in Lewiston, his heart filled with uncertainty as he contemplated his next steps. He harbored no concrete plans, save for one burning desire: to see Mary Johnston once more. Though plagued by doubt and apprehension, he felt compelled to seek her out, unsure of how she would receive him but unwilling to let fear deter him from trying.

The times had changed since he last traveled in this area aboard the Peggy. There were noticeable signs of military buildup, especially on the American side. The fields around Lewiston and Lewiston Heights were whitened with the pitched tents of the many soldiers gathered for the coming storm. There was a similar whitening at Fort Niagara, Schlossing and Black Rock. Overlooking the shores of the Niagara River, he saw the batteries of twenty-four pounders, aimed and ready to release their deadly shot into the heart of Queenston. Moored along the shoreline was a large flotilla of boats, capable of carrying at least thirty men each. Sailors, skilled in navigating quick flowing waters, stood nearby, awaiting the order to cross.

As Nathan arrived in the Lewiston area on the morning of October 10th, he found himself amidst a flurry of activity and anticipation. Conversations with the soldiers and militia revealed the extent of their dedication and resolve. They had traveled from regions as far-reaching as New York and Pennsylvania to join in the invasion of Upper Canada. With over eight thousand troops gathered, optimism ran high and talk of completing their forefathers' mission echoed through the air.

"We will drive the British from every corner of this country," one officer proclaimed with fervor. "We will set the people free from British tyranny."

Yet, despite the fervent optimism pulsing through the American forces, a stark contrast awaited across the Niagara River in Upper Canada. Here, amid President Madison's declaration of war in June, General Brock grappled with the grim reality of limited resources and outnumbered troops. Aware of the importance of maintaining British dominance on Lake Ontario, Brock had petitioned Governor Prevost for reinforcements, only to be met with denial. The key to securing a vigorous defense of the Niagara Region lay in securing control of the waterways, yet Brock's plea to attack and secure Sacket's Harbor, the American naval shipyard, fell on deaf ears.

As Nathan observed the stark contrast between the optimism of the American forces and the sobering reality faced by General Brock and his troops, he couldn't help but feel a sense of foreboding lingering in the air. The stage was set for a confrontation that would test the resolve of both sides and shape the course of the war to come.

Regardless of how he felt, a general cannot show pessimism and doubt among his troops. Brock became tireless in shoring up the defenses on the Niagara frontier. He had ordered that troops in Kingston and Amherstburg be dispatched immediately to Niagara. After the capture of Fort Detroit in August, he brought their armaments with him. Batteries were erected with captured cannons. Two thousand muskets were distributed among the militia and a system of beacon lights were built between Port Albino, Lundy's Lane and as far inland as Pelham Heights. Brock became known, by both friend and foe, as "he who guards never sleeps". He continued to strengthen the militia, organize the regular troop, and secure the help of the natives for this coming conflict.

Amidst General Brock's strategic preparations and his anticipation of an invasion at either Fort Erie or Fort Niagara, the small contingent of troops stationed at Queenston remained on edge. Despite Brock's belief that the battle would not begin at Queenston, the soldiers braced themselves for any eventuality, ready to defend the flanks as needed.

Meanwhile, Nathan stood on the shoreline at Lewiston, discreetly observing the movements of both armies with the eyeglass he had brought from the Peggy. Fully aware of the heightened alertness among the troops, he took precautions to shield himself behind a boulder, careful not to draw attention to his presence. With his elbows resting on the rock and the eyeglass in hand, Nathan scanned the horizon with a sense of purpose. He knew precisely what, or rather who, he was searching for amidst the flurry of activity along the shoreline.

Sharpening the focus, he found the spot where the Peggy had moored months before. The only movement near the docks was soldiers moving about, glancing at the eastern shores of the Niagara River. Followed by the sightline along the walkway that he had taken with Mary, Nathan found the Hamilton estate, still looming large over the town of Queenston. He had some alternative motive, which is why he didn't want to be a "watcher". He wanted to know if Mary was still there in the house and that she was safe.

Pausing briefly, he slid the eyeglass across the face of the house. Finding where he knew that the study was, he drew a deep breath. Standing by the window was Mary, looking out at something. He tried to follow her gaze with the eyeglass as he searched the lower areas of Queenston, but saw nothing. As his eyeglass focused once more on where he saw her, the lens reflected the sun's rays with a flash of light. Mary quickly stepped away and closed the curtains. Nathan stood for a moment and then climbed his way back up the steep cliffs towards Lewiston.

Chapter 9

General Van Rensselaer had set the date for the invasion by the American forces on October 11 at 3 am. The soldiers were preparing for this moment, drilling, and marching in battle array. He wanted his soldiers to maintain their military discipline. He also wanted to display his military superiority over any army that the British might have. Hull may have been duped at Fort Detroit into surrendering. Van Rensselaer would not be so easily taken by his enemies.

Throughout the day, the weather took a turn for the worse. The northeast winds brought an icy chill as they increased in intensity. By evening, they had reached gale force. Everything was soaked by the chilling winds and rain as they blew relentlessly. Amidst the howling winds, the soldiers struggled to stay warm in their tents. The driving rains made the roads impassable, as sentries cursed at their luckless fate of being assigned guard duty.

In the best of circumstances, crossing the Niagara River posed formidable challenges. With currents racing at six knots per hour, the waters surged from the falls and coursed through the gorge. Though a ferry crossing had been workable during times of peace, only the most adept navigators dared to brave these perilous waters. Despite sailors prepared to ferry their bateaux across the rushing currents, mastering the Niagara demanded a specialized skill set possessed by few. Van Rensselaer found himself confronted with a decision he had hoped to avoid, yet grappling with both the British and the unpredictable weather left him with no choice but to postpone the invasion until conditions improved.

Maintaining secrecy regarding invasion plans proved challenging amidst prevailing confidence in the mission's success. Information inevitably seeped through the ranks, reaching receptive ears. Somehow, Nathan learned of the invasion's scheduled commencement in the early hours of the 11th. Helpless to alter the impending course of events, he watched with a sinking feeling as the tide of troops loomed closer. Casting his gaze across the river once more, Nathan couldn't shake the unsettling realization that Mary lay directly in the path of the impending onslaught.

Nathan stood for a moment, almost in a valley of indecision. Should he not just let the events unfold as they ought? What could he do about it? His grandfather and father had weathered the onslaughts of the British during the last war and triumphed in the new America. Why not just head east and return to the home of his parents?

He found shelter, away from the biting cold, near the shores of the river. Wrapping his cloak tighter around his neck, he continued to wrestle with this decision that lay before him. He knew that if he crossed, he may also get caught in this military storm that was soon to break on the opposite shores. What should he do? Watching the large house opposite, he saw the curtain of an upper room move ever so slightly, illuminated by the flickering of a candle. Nathan knew what he must do. Mary may be loyal to King George, but this is not her fight, at least not a fight that she can survive. He must at least try to help her before the fight begins.

Nathan made his way along the riverbank, slipping often on the greasy rocks. He was looking for anything that he might find to cross this rushing river. It was difficult. The deluge of rain darkened the river before him as he shivered under its onslaught. Moving further along, he found a small boat that had been pulled onto shore. It had been turned over, with oars still tucked beneath the safety of its sides.

Wanting to make certain that he hadn't been followed, he waited for a moment, but all was quiet, except for the howling wind. Foe and friend alike sought shelter from the driving cold. Only the brave or foolish ventured to be in the open. He certainly didn't feel brave in these moments as he looked across the swirling waters.

Grabbing the boat by its side, he flipped it over. Taking the oars in one hand and dragging the boat with the other, he pulled it closer to the water's edge. The real challenge was whether he could keep the boat from flipping him into its icy waters or even come close to where he hoped he could land. Balancing himself with difficulty, he pushed the boat out into the rushing waters. This small boat was no Peggy, and this river was not like the last time he sailed upon it. The waters churned violently as he placed the oars in the locks and pulled with all his might.

The driving wind and the rushing rivers seemed, on this night, to be favorable towards Nathan. Though the river moved downward at a quick pace, the northeaster pushed its way up the river. With hard draws on the oars, Nathan slowly edged his way towards the shores of Upper Canada. The challenge was to keep the boat pointed towards the shoreline, without turning downwards. He had known hard waters before, but this was testing all his skill and strength. A ten-minute crossing became, for Nathan, an hour, but with one last pull, the bow nestled on the shoreline. He wanted to lean back and catch his breath, but this was not the time or place. He had other business to attend to and must be about this business before another storm breaks upon these shores.

Pulling the boat onto the shoreline, he stopped for a moment to get his bearings. His muscles ached with the strain of trying to make land in these hard waters. He had drifted farther down the Niagara River than he had hoped, but not as far as he could have. Taking but a moment to rest, he soon made his way up the hills that surrounded Queenston.

Chapter 10

Queenston stood as a pivotal hub for both commerce and strategic positioning. Its principal street traversed the village, extending toward Fort George and Niagara, while York Road connected Queenston to St. Davids. Notably, Portage Road, initially established as a trading route by Robert Hamilton and his associates, facilitated commerce between Queenston and Chippewa.

Amidst the challenges of Nathan's journey to Lewiston's water edge, the contrasting terrain between the two locations became apparent. While the cliffs on the American side offered scant shelter with their sheer steepness, Queenston's landscape unfolded in a gentler ascent. The hills rose gradually, cloaked in dense foliage that provided both concealment and refuge for Nathan as he navigated their heights.

Nathan, on his journey with the Peggy, had only known the area to the west of Queenston, near the docks. Yet while there, he had seen the wagons, loaded with Hamilton's wares, move slowly along an upper road.

Maybe that is why Nathan risked taking the road into Queenston. Trying to maneuver his way through the forest would be time and labor intensive. Besides, he reasoned, with this driving wind and rainstorm, very few people would be on the road. Making his way up the hill, he found the road, already muddied by the rain. He could only hope not to be challenged as he made his way towards Queenston.

Night had settled upon the village of Queenston. There were no candle lights flickering in the windows. There was no movement of any kind. Even the dogs had taken shelter. All but the weather was silent.

Nathan stood at the edge of the town, unsure of what to do next. Should he go to the Hamilton house and awaken Mary? Should he just keep watch? Before he crossed, there were rumors that the invasion would be delayed until the weather cleared. Maybe waiting would be the better course of action.

Moving through the village, he carefully stayed in the shadows until he arrived at the docks. He looked closely across the river for any troop movement, but there was nothing. Finding a dry place, he decided that for now, he would keep watch and wait. It wasn't long before the strain of the day overtook him, and he was soon fast asleep.

He was awakened with a hand on his shoulder. Two soldiers of the 49th stood over him, muskets pointed towards this startled stranger.

"Who are you and why are you here?" bellowed the corporal.

"I came last night from St. Davids, but it was late and there was no place for me to stay." He hoped his face wouldn't betray the lie as he stared into the corporal's eyes.

"We dislike strangers in our midst. These are troubled times. What do you do in St. Davids? Is there anyone here who can vouch for you?" the corporal pressed.

"I have done business with Mary Johnson, the one living in the big house."

"We know who she is. An honorable woman. You better not have any ill thoughts towards her." He leaned in, dropping the musket barrel on Nathan's chest.

"I do not. I am here to do business and will announce my presence to her. When done, I will return to where I came from," he said, as he got to his feet.

"Make sure you do. We know who comes and goes in our village. Strangers are not welcome, so be quick about your business and leave."

Nathan moved away from the two soldiers and trudged back towards the Hamilton house.

The morning light had chased away the darkness, but not the howling winds or driving rain. As he moved away from his dry place, he had only one thought on his mind.

"How can I speak with Mary about what may happen to her if she stays?"

Nathan had braved many waters and known many dangers as a sailor. Yet he felt afraid and almost indecisive about what to do next.

This was new to him. He was always quick to size up a situation, decide upon a course of action, and move forward. Maybe it was the issues of his heart that were not as clear to him. Maybe it was more than rescuing this woman from impending danger. Could he be afraid of rejection, of being cast off like a ship set loose from its moorings?

Either way, he must decide. He can return to the far shores from which he came. Or he can do what he set out to do and speak with Mary.

He chose the latter. If she rejects him, fine. At least he will have done what he knew within himself was the right thing to do.

Nathan moved towards the Hamilton house. The pathway was now covered with mud and washed down debris as he slipped and struggled to find his footing. Slowly and carefully, he edged ever nearer, until he finally arrived at the front door. He thought he had seen a curtain move ever so slightly as he neared and knew that it was pointless to go back now.

Squeezing his hand into a ball, he knocked as if he was trying to awaken the entire village of Queenston. Only silence answered his knock.

The rain had now again increased in intensity. It no longer came straight down, but was driven sideways by the wind. Nathan pulled his jacket tighter around his neck and knocked once more, this time even louder than the first. The handle of the door moved slightly as the door cracked opened.

"Yes, who is there? What do you want?" Mary whispered.

"It's Nathan, Nathan Douglas. I was here with the Peggy a few months back. I need to talk to you. Can I come in?" he shouted, afraid that the wind would drown out his words.

"I have no business with you," she said. "No more cargo has been ordered by me, and no ships are expected, especially not in this weather."

"Yes, I'm aware. I'm not here for that," Nathan replies. "I need to talk to you. Can I please come in? If you want me to leave, I will. Just let me come in and talk."

Mary seemed to hesitate for a moment and then, stepping back from the door, she left it open enough so that Nathan could squeeze through. With a firm shove, he closed the door.

She just stood there, looking at him. Both seemed unsure what to do next.

"Don't move. I will get something for you to dry yourself with."

Nathan was thankful to be away from the icy chills of the driving wind and rain. As he stood there, his body shook - maybe from being cold, maybe from fear of rejection. In the other room, he could see the glow of a fireplace. He longed to move towards its warmth, but Mary had specifically told him to wait there. It was not a request. He knew how to obey orders and he wasn't about to disobey this one.

Mary returned shortly, laden with some towels that Nathan could use to dry off with. She was only the supplier of the towels. Drying himself was his task, and she was not about to help him. Tossing them to him, she stood back and waited. Even as he ran the towels over his face and hair, he still looked like a wet puppy. With a sigh, she told him to wait there while she gets some dry things for him to wear.

"If you stay in those clothes, you will get sick and you will not come into the house looking like that. Stay here and do not move."

A short time later, Mary returned with a man's trousers and shirt.

"Take your shoes and socks off. Wipe your feet well and you can go into that room to change. These belonged to Mr. Hamilton and may be large, but it's all I have. When you are done, bring your wet things into the study by the fire. You remember how to find it, don't you?"

Nathan could only nod as they parted ways, she to the study and he to change. Carefully rolling his wet clothes, he squeezed out the water into the towels. Making his way to the study, he saw Mary, sitting where he last saw her, behind that large wooden desk.

She looked up at him and couldn't help but laugh. He looked so small in Mr. Hamilton's clothes, as they sagged awkwardly on his body.

Nathan didn't care. In fact, he was enjoying the moment. It was good to be in Mary's company, even if he still felt out of place. He walked over to the blazing fire and carefully laid out his damp clothes. Then he took his place in the same chair he sat in, when last in this room.

Outside, he could hear the thunderous roar of the storm clouds as they clapped their fury across the lightened sky. He could only think that they were nothing compared to what awaited them in the coming days.

Chapter 11

General Van Rensselaer had ordered his troops to stand down as they awaited the end of this storm. They had been gathering since September for this coming conflict and were tired of "standing down". The regular troops had arrived from places in New York and Pennsylvania. Farmers had left family and farms behind to join the militia. The final reaping of their harvests was left to their families, thinking that this invasion wouldn't take too much of their time. The natives soon needed to return to their hunting grounds to secure winter provisions.

These troops had gathered for one purpose: to invade the lands of the opposing armies and begin the drive to remove Britain completely from its North American holdings. But the storm of the11th had other plans as it continued to rage into the next day, still making the crossing risky.

The American officers gathered together on the morning of the 12th, in the rather large tent of Van Rensselaer. They continued to develop their battle plans for when, not if, the weather changes in their favor. Recent military successes by the Americans had bolstered the confidence of the troops that now is the time to invade. Two small British vessels stationed near Fort Erie had been destroyed only days earlier. Spies reported that General Brock had left the Niagara area for Detroit. Without his commanding presence, the British would easily fall into confusion and defeat.

But Brock had not left. The reports were false. He continued to meet with his officers, traveling continually across Niagara and preparing for what he knew was soon to happen. Truly, "he who guards never sleeps."

The storms abated on the night of the 12th. The rain still fell, but the winds would no longer prevent the boats from crossing the Niagara River. General Brock had prepared his troops for landings at either Fort Niagara or Fort Erie. He reasoned that if the Americans could land at either or both places, they could turn the flanks of the British troops and catch them in the center. He had strengthened Fort George and Fort Erie, leaving only a small garrison to protect the center at Queenston. Having gone to bed at midnight, he fell fast asleep, unaware that they were other plans in place that would have dire consequences for himself.

Fully prepared for battle, the remaining troops stationed at Fort Niagara and Schlosser were ordered by General van Rensselaer to be moved to Lewiston under cover of darkness. The final preparations had been made. The invasion would begin on that night, Tuesday, October 13, at 3 am.

Nathan found himself seated across from Mary in the study of Robert

Hamilton, his thoughts swirling as he sought the right words to express. Memories flooded back to the day when he first laid eyes on her, walking towards him from this very house. She still captivated him, just as she did then. In the room's quiet, they both sat, the weight of unspoken words hanging heavy in the air, waiting for the moment to break the silence.

"Thank you for letting me come in. I needed to speak with you."
She stayed silent, waiting for him to continue. It was rather humorous watching this
sailor, this cocky sailor, struggle to find the words that he wanted to say. But he better hurry. The storm will end, and he cannot stay here.

"Mary, can I call you Mary?" he asked, without waiting for a response. "You may have heard that the Americans have declared war against Britain and are, as of this moment, gathering across the river to await the order to invade."

"I know that President Madison has declared war. I have watched from the upper windows the troops gathering and the growing tents," she said, with little feeling. "General Brock has been no stranger to our village."

"Why would you come back here, since you are an American sailor?" Mary asked. "All I need to do is find a soldier and you would be arrested. These are troubled times. There are very few people we trust and strangers that we trust less. You would be wise to slip out while you can and make your way back from where you came."

Mary turned slightly in her chair as she stared out the window and across the waters, towards the shores of Lewiston.

"I came to warn you that the battle is about to happen anytime now. If you stay here, you will be caught up in the battle and either captured or killed, or …", Nathan said, in almost a whisper. He did not want to think of those possibilities, but he knew that soldiers, unrestrained, could do things they would not do otherwise.

"I have seen the troops and walked through their camps. These are not just regular soldiers, but also militia and Indians. There are over eight thousand troops gathered to invade. How many does General Brock have? Maybe a thousand. Maybe two thousand. He is outnumbered and outgunned. The Americans have set up twenty-four pounders at Fort Gray, above the heights of Lewiston, aimed towards this village. I have seen them. There are two eighteen-pounders aimed at the redan, above the heights of Queenston. There are mortars and six-pounders along the river's edge. They have one goal in mind, the establishing of a foothold in Niagara before winter sets in, even if it means destroying Queenston. You cannot stay here," he said, as he leaned forward in his chair. "You must find safety."

"Where would I go?" she whispered. "Who would look after this place? If it is as you say, I will ask the American officers to allow me to continue to stay here and manage the affairs of Mr. Hamilton."

"There will be no affairs of Mr. Hamilton left to manage." He was feeling more exasperated.

"The Americans will become the sole owners of everything. Even if they let you stay here, where do you think the officers will stay?" he pressed. "They have been living in tents and you have plenty of room in this house. You will be moved to a small room as they take over full control of this house. You will be required to feed and tend to their every need. Can't you see this?" he now said in full voice, almost shouted.

Mary sat, as if completely absorbed in her own thoughts. She knew he was probably right about what he was saying. But how could she just abandon her post? If they came, there was nothing she could do to stop them. If they didn't come and she left the house unattended, there are still those who would steal from them..

The rain pounded against the panes of glass as the winds circled the house, searching for any place they might enter. Mary pushed herself back from the desk, placing two more logs in the fireplace. They sat there in silence as they listened to the crackling of the fire and the howling of the wind.

"Regardless, nothing will happen as long as this storm continues," she said. "The waters are too treacherous at the best of times. They won't risk their lives in this."

He could only nod. There was no sense trying to reason with Mary any further. Her mind was made up. There was nothing he could do to change that, at least for the moment.

Nathan got up from where he was sitting and walked over to get his clothes. By now they had dried enough that he could put them back on and get out of these clothes, of a much larger Mr. Hamilton. Mary stood near the outer edge of the fireplace as he walked by her.

"Another time and another place," he thought to himself. "She is truly a fine woman. Stubborn, yes, but very fine."

With a nod, he turned as he made his way to change.

"Where will you go?" she asked. "You won't walk five minutes before you are as wet as when you came."

"I'll find some place dry. Maybe where I spent the night before I came here." He tried to convince himself that this was the best plan of action. He had no plan beyond speaking with Mary. He knew what the soldiers said when they woke him with muskets in his chest. Truthfully, he did not know where to go. He had barely made it across the river the first time, and he sure didn't want to try it again with this storm raging.

"You can't go back out there with the weather like it is. There is a bed in the back room where you changed. You can stay there, but only until the storm passes. Then you must go. Are we clear on this?"

"Yes, thank you for your kindness, but please, think about what I just said." Nathan left the study, making his way to the back room. Only this time, he had a little more spring to his step. The storm may come, but for the moment, both are safe.

Chapter 12

Nathan quickly changed into his own clothes as he gathered up Mr. Hamilton's, bringing them back to the study. Mary had moved to an arm back chair. She motioned for him to take the other chair, though she had positioned it so there was a small table between them. On that table, Mary had carefully laid out some bread, cheese, and a pot of tea.

"I assume you haven't eaten for some time, so I took the liberty," she said, rather sheepishly. It was as if she had invited Nathan to her private tea party in this vast mansion.

"Thank you. I have had nothing since yesterday and yes, I am rather hungry." He leaned in to take the food. Suddenly, he stopped. This was not the galley of the Peggy, where every man was for himself. He at least needed to show Mary that he had some manners.

"Please, after you," he said, leaning back and waiting for her. She daintily placed a piece of bread on her plate, cheese beside it, and then poured herself a cup of tea. She then poured Nathan a cup and leaned back, waiting.

They were like two children caught in the game of one-upmanship. They knew it and, with a laugh, they both ate what was before them.

"What happened to the Peggy?" she asked.

"She is docked at Oswego. When the war was declared, it was no longer safe for us to sail these waters. The owners were already in negotiations with the navy to sell her sister ship, the Diana, to be used as a warship. She had been taken to Sacket's Harbor, but I think the Peggy is still where we left her."

"Will you go back to her if they also use her as a warship? Maybe join the navy. After all, you know her very well."

"No, I am not wanting to join the navy or the army. My family had enough of the last war, and I do not want to take up arms against anyone. I just want to sail the lake like I used to, but that will not happen now."

"Why don't you go back to Burlington?" she asked. "Your parents are there, and it is far enough away from this conflict."

"No, it won't be safe either. No one wants the war in the northeast. Trade is good between the two countries. Montreal has been a great place for my folks to ship their goods, but, like the last war, there are others who see it differently. No, war has come there as well, and no one can escape it." He had this far-off look, as if he was searching for something, anything, but war.

"Ah, the last war," she sighed. "I only know the stories that my grandparents told me. Dad doesn't want to talk about it. Was your family always from Burlington?"

"No," and then he caught himself. He had only told her part of his story when he last sat in this office. There was another part that intertwined with hers. If he was to tell her, knowing how much her family had suffered, well, he was just unsure how she would react. His grandfather, once a friend of her grandfather, had put politics ahead of friendship and their lives were irrevocably changed.

"What is it?" she asked, as he stared out the window. "You can tell me?"

"If I were to tell you the story of my family, I don't think you would like us. In fact, I am afraid that you may hate us, and me, because it is not pretty," he quietly answered her.

Mary tried not to show any emotion, but it seeped out on the edges as she shifted in her chair. She had lowered her emotional defenses, relaxing around this sailor, but maybe all was not what she had hoped it would be. Maybe he couldn't be trusted. After all, he was still an American and her family had left all that behind.

He noticed the slight change within her. Should he continue with his story? Would it be best if he just left? As he sat there, the silence had become awkward between them. She was waiting for him to say something. He was not sure that he wanted to say anything. Finally, he took a deep breath. If there was to be any hope of a relationship, it had to be built on trust and not lies. Nathan looked her in the eyes as he began.

"No, we weren't always from Burlington. My parents moved there after the War of Independence. I was born there, but my grandparents were from Scotland, like yours. Times were hard for them in their homeland and so, after they married, they wanted a new life for them and their family. They left Scotland for Albany."

Nathan waited to see what Mary would do, but she remained stoic as she listened.

"Your grandparents lived outside of Albany on a farm," he continued. "My grandparents lived in Albany. They had a small house and my grandfather had learned from his father how to be a merchant. He sold and traded goods. Maybe some of the produce your grandfather brought into Albany was sold by him. I don't know. All I know is that when the British started demanding that we take their troops into our home and board them, something changed in my grandfather."

Nathan's mouth had suddenly gone dry. Reaching down, he poured another cup of tea, took a deep drink, while glancing up at Mary, but she had not moved or changed expression. He had this gut feeling that maybe she knew where this was going.

"His desire was for the British to be gone, gone from his home, gone from Albany, and gone from the colonies. He had left Scotland to start a new life and that new life did not include being under British rule. My grandfather spoke to whoever would listen. If he had traded with your family, he probably would have spoken to them as well."

Nathan again paused.

"How much more do you want to know?" he asked.

Mary only nodded.

"It was important to my grandfather that only those loyal to the cause of independence be allowed to hold office or have land. General Brock, under Governor Prevost's orders, has done the same thing. I may not agree with their decisions, but I understand why they did what they did."

Nathan took a deep breath. "My grandfather joined the Safety Committee. I know this committee forced your family to flee. I don't know what to say except that I am sorry it happened.

Mary waited before standing. "Thank you for your honesty in telling me this. This makes it impossible for us to continue to do business or be friends. You are welcome to stay as I promised, but I would like you gone in the morning."

He will do as she asked and be gone by morning.

Chapter 13

The early mornings of the 13th showed promising signs that the storm had blown itself out. Despite the cloudy sky and lingering mist, the wind had calmed down. This General van Rensselaer was looking for. At midnight, he summoned his officers to his tent, reviewed the final battle strategies, and commanded the invasion to begin at 3 am.

A well-designed battle plan was necessary in any war if there was to be hope of success, especially in the early stages. It was important that they protect their landing forces by the river's edge, silence the opposing guns and capture the strategic points on the enemy's ground. This meant that they must capture the docks at Queenston, contain the small British force stationed there, silence the gun at the redan and establish a strong military presence on Queenston Heights, before any British troops can be reinforced, either from Fort George or Fort Chippewa.

General van Rensselaer had planned to lead the advance guard, but when Colonel Chrystie arrived, he refused to relinquish his command. It was agreed that Chrystie would lead a column of 300 regular troops and Van Rensselaer a column of 300 militia. The advance guard was carefully selected from among the troops gathered. These were tasked with securing the landing area at Queenston.

The British guns at the redan and the river's edge needed to be silenced. Forty skilled artillerymen from Fort Niagara were tasked with silencing these guns. Once the positions were secured, these artillerymen, with an attachment of engineers, would then fortify the captured positions.

Following them were to be four companies of the 13th United States infantry; then 550 regulars led by Colonel Fenwick and Major Mullany; then 550 militia until the entire division of the 16th, 17th, 18th, 19th and 20th regiments of the New York militia.

The battle plans called for 4000 troops, 1500 of them regulars to be ferried over on seven trips.

By 2:30 am, the advance guard had assembled by the bateaux, poised for the imminent invasion. At 3 am sharp, the command to advance was issued. Within minutes, 300 troops, under the leadership of General van Rensselaer, disembarked onto the shores of Queenston, their presence unnoticed by any sentries. However, Colonel Chrystie's boat struggled against the strong currents of the Niagara River, forcing it to return to Lewiston to regroup. In the interim, Van Rensselaer assumed full command, swiftly organizing his troops and ordering them to form up before advancing toward the enemy.

Meanwhile, back in Queenston, neither Nathan nor Mary found restful sleep after their tense encounter in Robert Hamilton's study. Nathan's revelation regarding his grandfather's role in bringing hardship upon Mary's family weighed heavily on her heart. The betrayal she felt was deep, stirring emotions of hurt and anger. How could
Nathan, knowing the pain his family had caused, dared to return uninvited? Mary's family had left their homeland in Scotland to seek a new life in Albany, only to be shattered by the actions of Nathan's grandfather. The move to Queenston and St. Davids was a fresh start, but it came at a great cost, with her grandparents succumbing to the hardships and her mother perishing in childbirth. The maternal love she yearned for was lost forever, leaving her father to rebuild their shattered lives alone. Mary couldn't fathom forgiving of such a betrayal. As she lay awake, she hoped fervently that Nathan would depart before her awakening, longing for a day free from his presence forever.

As Nathan lay there, lost in his own thoughts of what might have been, a loud gunshot was heard, coming from somewhere near the river. Nathan jumped out of bed, quickly dressed and moved towards the study area of the house. Peering out the window by the river's edge, he saw a large contingent of soldiers wearing the blue colors of the American army. The invasion had begun.

Nathan ran to the stairwell that led to the upstairs bedrooms, where Mary lay.

"Mary, leave. The American army has landed on the shores of Queenston and will soon make their way up the riverbanks into the village. You cannot stay here, at least until the battle is over, whatever way it goes," he shouted. "Please, Mary, time is of the essence."

Mary descended the stairs to the study, her mind buzzing with uncertainty. She couldn't shake her distrust of Nathan, yet she knew personal feelings couldn't cloud her judgment in this critical moment. "What do we do?" she asked, her voice betraying a flicker of hope that the safety of the Hamilton house might shield them from the chaos unfolding outside. But deep down, she knew it was a futile wish, a fleeting hope that would soon be dashed.

Outside the Hamilton house, Captain Dennis sprang into action upon receiving the sentry's alert. With swift efficiency, he rallied his forty-six troopers and a handful of militias, swiftly moving toward the river. Across the water, the Americans remained disorganized and unprepared. Seizing the opportunity, the British forces formed a battle line, their movements precise and coordinated. With deadly accuracy, they unleashed their first volley upon the unsuspecting American soldiers. Amid the chaos, General Van Rensselaer bore the brunt of the onslaught, being struck multiple times as he and his troops scrambled back toward the shoreline in disarray.

As Mary grappled with her thoughts in the study, a sudden eruption of noise shattered her indecision. The thunderous roar of the twenty-six pounders reverberated through the air, signaling the onset of hostilities. With the British troops effectively trapping the American army by the river's edge, the artillerymen wasted no time in redirecting their fire toward the musket flashes of the enemy. However, their targeting was indiscriminate, and the rounds and grape shots unleashed by the cannons now rained down upon the village of Queenston, including the Hamilton house situated directly in their line of fire.

The deafening crash of collapsing walls jolted Mary from her stupor, dispelling any lingering hopes of the house providing protection. Realization struck her with chilling clarity: they were vulnerable to the merciless onslaught of the enemy. With no other option but to flee for her life, Mary's thoughts turned to escape, clinging to the slim hope of returning later—if anything remained.

"Where do we go?" she asked Nathan. "Where will we be safe?"

"The village is no longer safe. We must work our way towards the east side of the village, towards that large oak tree that stands tall on the outskirts. You remember where it is. As the Peggy would come towards Queenston, I knew we were getting close when I saw the tree. If we get separated, make for the tree and I will meet you there."

Mary moved towards the side door of the estate, grabbing her coat and wrapping herself in its warmth. Mary bravely stepped into the chilly night, joining Nathan to confront an unknown future, uncertain if they would even see another day.

Chapter 14

General Brock was awakened by the loud sounds of cannon fire as he lay asleep in the barracks at Fort George. He had met with James McDonnell, former attorney general of the province and James Givias of the Indian department, till midnight as they continued to prepare for the coming invasion. They knew it was coming. They just did not expect it to come where it did.

Captain Dennis and Lieutenant Crowther of the 41st kept the Americans pinned by the shores of the river. Van Rensselaer had been taken back to Lewiston to have his wounds attended to. The command for the American troops fell upon Captain Wool of the 13th, inexperienced in the art of war.

For two hours, the American forces seemed to be content to remain hidden by the banks of the river, occasionally firing their weapons but never finding their intended targets. Yet the artillery was not so aimless. They continued to unleash their fury on the village of Queenston and soon houses and gardens were leveled. The Hamilton estate, once standing stately, was now reduced to a pile of rubble. No one was safe from this barrage.

More American troops climbed into their respective bateaux to cross the Niagara River. Some made it to their appointed landing. Others did not. Colonel Fenwick, seeking to bring more artillery by bateaux, drifted with the current and was met by British troops, himself being maimed in the face. Yet those who made the landing soon doubled Wool's forces, though no officer of superior rank came to assume control of the American forces.

The British gun in the redan continued to throw its armament into the river crossing, seldom hitting any targets but creating doubt, especially among the militia, of anyone seeking to cross while the eighteen pounder was still operational.

General Brock dressed quickly, still believing that the attack at Queenston was a ruse and the major attack would occur, either at Fort Niagara or Fort Erie. Leaving his major force in Fort George, he rode out with Lieutenant Colonel McDonnell and Major Glegg towards the sounds of the cannons. Gathering the militia at Brown's and Field's Point, he left only enough men to man the batteries. Each began the "quick march" towards the sounds of battle.

The morning light had chased away the darkness, revealing four more boats making their way across the river towards the shores of Queenston.

Captain Dennis, needing reinforcements, ordered his bugler to call the troops manning the battery on the redan to join forces with him in the village, leaving behind only enough men to continue firing their weapon into the river's edge at Lewiston.

As the chaos of battle unfolded around them, Nathan and Mary hurriedly retreated from the crumbling remains of the Hamilton estate, seeking refuge from the relentless onslaught of artillery fire. With each deafening blast, Mary's heart sank further, witnessing the destruction of the once-grand dwelling that held so many cherished memories. Tears streamed down her cheeks as she grappled with a mix of emotions — gratitude for their safety mingled with a seething anger at being once again thrust into a war she never wished for.

Meanwhile, on the American side, Captain Wool, despite his wounds, swiftly devised a plan to break free from the perilous position along the shoreline. Recognizing the urgency of the situation, he ordered a hundred men to remain behind and engage the British forces, while the rest of the troops embarked on a daring ascent along a fisherman's trail. Their aim: to outflank the enemy's redan and seize the high ground.

Nathan stood beside Mary as he watched the shells tearing through the estate where, only moments earlier, they had been. He listened to her sobs and longed to reach out. As they stood there, he sought to place his hand in hers, sought to pull her close, that he might console her, sought to bring her comfort in her moment of grief.

"Don't touch me. Your family destroyed us once and are now seeking to destroy us again."

"This is not my family," he said. "We are not seeking to destroy you or anyone."

"Don't lie to me," she hissed through clenched teeth. "You are an American and it is the Americans who have declared war, the Americans who have invaded our land, and the Americans who are now destroying my home and the homes of the people I love. So don't give me your lies that this is not you. You are them and this is you."

There was nothing that Nathan could say. She was right about the war. It was sweeping all over its path and no one was safe from its ways.

"I need to check on the Secords to see if Laura and her family are safe," she blurted. "You can stay here and join your friends, or you can come with me. At this moment, I don't care." She turned and made her way towards the east side of Queenston.

The Secord home was a small dwelling that was home to James and Laura, along with their five children, ranging in ages from 2 to 13. They had built this white paneled dwelling in 1803 to accommodate their growing family. James, a merchant by trade, had also established a store on his property. By the time the war broke out, they had made a pleasant home and a successful business. The war was about to change all that for them.

Mary and Nathan made their way towards the Secord home, careful to stay off the main road and away from the soldiers on either side. Nathan was careful not to be mistaken for an American soldier. As they neared the home, no one was to be seen, no candles lit any window. Mary drew near and knocked.

"Laura, it's Mary. Are you there? I want to make sure that you and your family are safe." She placed her face near the door. She did not want to be heard by anyone but the Secords.

After a brief moment, the door cracked. Seeing that no one else was near, Laura quickly pulled them in and shut the door, securing it after them.

"Are you okay, Mary?" Laura quickly glanced at Nathan, wondering who this might be with her friend.

"I heard the cannon fire, and I knew, I just knew, that the Hamilton estate was being hit. Were you in it? I am so glad to see you safe." She wrapped her arms around Mary, pulling her close.

"Yes, we got out just before the house was hit. I can't tell you how scared I was to hear the sounds and feel the explosions.

"Everything is lost." Mary broke into deep sobs as she wept in Laura's arms.

"But you are here, safe and for that I am grateful. Who is this with you?" she asked. Nathan was still standing near the closed door.

"This is Nathan, the sailor who had brought supplies to us a few months ago," she offered, without looking at him.

"American? And you trust him? Mary, these are Americans who have declared war and have attacked our beloved village. How can you trust him?"

"I know. He came to warn me that there was an attack coming. He was there when the house was hit."

"He was alone with you in that vast house at the Hamilton estate? Mary, I thought I knew you better."

"It's not like that. We only met the day he sailed here with the Peggy. There is nothing between us and there never will be anything between us. For now, he is helping," she offered, with no emotion.

"Where is James?" Mary asked. "Is he at the store? Who is looking after you and helping you?"

"James had joined the 1st Lincoln militia earlier this year and was quickly promoted to the rank of sergeant. I love a man in a uniform, and he looked so good. He left early this morning to join Captain Dennis when the first shots rang out. I hope he is safe."

Laura had this look about her that only wives of soldiers could ever understand.

"I hope so as well," Mary offered. "I'm sure that he will be okay."

The artillery fire continued to pour into the village of Queenston. The grapeshot tore through orchards and gardens, destroying everything in their path.

"You can't stay here. It's not safe for you or the children," Mary said, with more urgency.

"Where would we go? Where could we go? Your house is no longer. The houses in the village are being ripped apart. They haven't reached us yet and I hope to God they don't, but where would we go?" she asked.

Nathan still stood by the doorway, a silent listener to the conversation but ever alert to the surrounding sounds.

"We are hoping to make it to the old oak tree. You know, the one on the outskirts of the village. We should be safe, away from the opposing armies."

"Would we not be safer here?" Laura asked. "After all, who would harm a mother with her five children? What could they do to us? Soldiers we are not. We have no weapons. We are harmless."

Mary glanced at Nathan, but he was without expression.

"Laura, these are not just soldiers but also militia and, with them, are Indians. I do not need to remind you what can happen when there are no officers around to instill order and discipline. Think of your children. Especially think of Mary and Charlotte, young ladies. For their safety, leave." Mary's voice was quiet, not wishing to alarm anyone, especially the children.

The morning was still early, but the children had now gathered by the fireplace: Mary, with little Apollonia, Charlotte, and Charles. Harriet, the eldest child was waiting, wanting to know from her mother whether everything would be okay.

"You are right. Can you help us get ready?"

"Yes. Come, children. Let's get dressed. You need to get your warm clothes on and good shoes. We are going for a walk."

Mary took Harriet by her hand, as they helped each get ready for the day that lay ahead, a day that would change their lives forever.

Chapter 15

General Brock arrived at the village of Queenston, covered with mud as his horse had galloped through the still wet roads towards the village. Following behind was McDonnell and the militia from Fort George. The men of the 49th shouted a loud cheer at his arrival. Brock was one of their own, having risen through the military ranks with the 49th.

Brock needed to survey the situation quickly. Riding his horse up to the redan, he dismounted and looked over the river towards Lewiston. In that moment, he knew he had assumed wrongly that the Americans would attack elsewhere. Battalion upon battalion of battle-ready troops were making their way towards the water's edge at Lewiston. Soon, there would be too many of them for the British to hold their position.

Without warning, shots were fired from above. The fisherman's trail had taken the Americans above the British, as the troops now made their way from the heights towards the redan. The British were now outflanked and caught between the enemy above and the enemy beneath. Grabbing the reins of his horse, Brock ordered his men, who by now were outnumbered, to retreat towards the village and join up with the other troops. As his men moved away from the eighteen pounder, they first spiked the gun to ensure that it could not be used against them.

The Americans quickly seized the redan, raising the American flag over their new possession. A loud shout could be heard from the across the river. Soldiers were now seen, clambering towards the river's edge, eager to take part in the victories now unfolding before them.

Dispatching a rider to Fort George, Brock ordered that General Sheaffe unleash his barrage of weaponry against Fort Niagara and to send the battalion companies of the 41st and the militia to Queenston. Time was of the essence. If the full contingent of the American army crossed and took position, he could not hold them.

Riding to the far end of the village, he found the company of the 49th awaiting orders. Without hesitation, he simply said, "Follow me, boys," until they reached the base of the hill that they were soon to ascend. "Take a breather, boys. You will need it in a few moments."

The Americans were now in possession of the redan, but the spiked cannon was of no use to them. They set up a mortar by the river's edge, hoping to hinder the British from moving to recapture the redan. Captain Dennis led the 49th Grenadiers and Chisholm's York militia as they prepared to retake the redan. Before the order to advance was given, Brock sent

Williams, with his own company and the whole of the militia, up a different route, seeking to outflank Wools and the Americans. But Wool, anticipating this move, ordered 150 of his own men to keep this from happening.

Seizing the moment, Brock ordered his men over the stone wall that had before offered them protection. Brandishing his sword, he led the charge up the hill towards the redan.

Lieutenant Colonel McDonnell led the companies that had just arrived from Brown's Point. With their troops now assembled, the British began their ascent towards the American forces.

Brock continued to press his soldiers to move forward. "Push on the York volunteers," he shouted to McDonnell. Williams, by now, was pressing against the flanks of the American troops.

The recent weather had made the hill slippery, as Brock and the grenadiers stumbled their way over the wet leaves.

Captain Wool had sent reinforcements to support his advance guard, and they now gathered in strength above the British troops, firing at will down the hill towards the British troops. Brock's line was broken as men retreated to the rear.

"This is the first time I have ever seen the 49th turn their backs!" Brock shouted angrily. Immediately, the 49th closed ranks, continuing their ascent up the slippery hill.

The hill provided sufficient cover for the American snipers, firing upon the British. As Brock brandished his sword, a bullet struck him in the wrist, but he continued to lead his men in front.

Suddenly, an American sniper stepped out from his cover and took aim at the British general. Brock's troops, seeing this, fired their own weapons, seeking to take out this sniper, but it was too late. General Isaac Brock was struck above the heart and died where he fell.

McDonnell spurred his horse forward and called on his troops to avenge their leader's death. McDonnell attacked from the thickets on the right and Williams on the flank. Soon the American troops fell into disorder and shrank away towards the river. The American troops who had seized control of the redan were now overrun and fled upwards, towards the crest of the hill.

Captain Wool took his stand on the verge of the cliffs overlooking Queenston Heights. The 6th United States infantry and other rifles soon joined him to take their stand.

Williams and Dennis had been injured in the battle. The only officer not injured was McDonnell, still atop his horse as he urged his York militia and the 49th of Foot to press forward. In his bright red vest, wearing the colors of a British officer, he drew the fire of the American troops. One bullet pierced his arm, another his leg as the bullets continued to find their mark. Suddenly, his horse reared up, tossing James McDonnell to the ground. With bullets flying everywhere, the horse stomped the ground, driving its hooves onto the body of this officer as he lay helpless beneath.

The British retreated down the hill towards Queenston, carrying the dead body of their General. Yet the Americans did not press the battle.

Dennis, though injured, refused to leave his command. Gathering his men at the far end of Queenston, he met with Crowther and his squad of Provincial artilleryman to determine how to move forward.

Other American troops were still waiting to cross at Lewiston. The river was now unopposed by the British and free for them to cross.

General van Rensselaer and Colonel Chrystie, from the heights of Lewiston, gave the order that Queenston Heights was to be immediately fortified. A six-pound field piece, complete with carriage and tumbril, was set up while the cannon at the redan, once spiked by the British, was now unspiked and free for use. Colonel Scott, crossing the river, took command of the American troops in Queenston and was quickly reinforced by the 6th, 23rd United States infantrymen, as well as the 2nd and 3rd artillery.

It seemed as if the American army had achieved their aim. A foothold now seemed to be established on the shores of the Niagara Region. But the British were not done yet.

Captain Derenzy led the 41st, while Holcroft planted his guns on the high ground below the village so that he might fire upon those who would seek to cross the river. But his guns were still too far away to be effective.

Captain Archibald Hamilton had grown up in this village. In fact, his father had been Robert Hamilton, owner of the Hamilton estate until his death. Archibald had played on these streets and knew every nook and cranny in the village of Queenstown. Finding Holcroft, Hamilton led him to the Hamilton estate, now in ruins from the American artillery. Bolstered by Derenzy and the 41st, their musket fire soon drove away the enemy's riflemen. Turning his guns towards the American batteries, he found he was too far distant, but not for the enemy ships still waiting to cross. With Holcroft and Derenzy manning their guns, no one dared to enter the waters of the Niagara River. The reinforcing of the American forces was over.

Colonel Scott had taken his position on the crest of Queenston Heights. The gun position was fortified; pickets were placed near the edge of the woods. But the British native allies' approach had gone undetected through the woods. The pickets were quickly silenced, with considerable American loss. The militia, panicking at the sound of their war cries, sought to make their way towards the shorelines of Queenston, hoping to find a bateau to take them back to safety.

Derenzy had sent word to General Sheaffe at Fort George of the situation at Queenston. Following the death of Brock, Sheaffe assumed command and ordered the troops stationed at Fort George and Fort Chippewa to proceed at once towards Queenston.

General Sheaffe was not about to make the same mistake as General Brock. Fortifying their position on the heights of Queenston, the Americans awaited the British to come over the crest of the hill and into their deadly weapons fire. The hill was slippery, the footing difficult. The Americans clearly had the upper hand as they waited.

The soldiers from Fort George were instructed to take an alternative route, which led them through St. Davids. A foot path would lead them up the escarpment and bring them in behind the American army. Undetected, the regulars and militia joined forces to begin the ending battle for Queenston Heights. James Secord, sergeant with the 1st Lincoln regiment, under John McEwen, also prepared for battle.

Chapter 16

Mary helped Laura with the children as they made their way towards safety. Nathan led the way, carefully choosing which path to take. They needed to hurry, as the sounds of musket and cannon fire seemed to be all around them.

"Quick, we need to get off the road. It's not safe for the children. Follow me," Nathan whispered.

Laura gave Mary a questioning look. Could they really trust this American, but what choice did they have? She knew it was not safe on the roadway. They needed to find shelter as they made their way out of Queenston.

Moving into the wooded area, nearing the outskirts of the village, Laura stopped and waited. What was it? Why had she stopped? Did she sense danger near to them?

"I need to go back to the house," she said. "I need to pack some clothes for James. The battle is soon to be over, and he is going to need a change of clothes. I need to go back."

"Laura, how can we? It would be too dangerous for the children to go back, and you can't go alone."

Mary had gently taken Laura by the arm, but to no avail. Laura pulled her arm free, turning to go.

"I need to go back. You don't understand, but I have to."

Laura's mind was set. She was going back. Yet it would be unwise if they all went back, and she certainly couldn't leave the children here alone in the woods.

"Nathan, I will stay with the children. Will you go with Laura and make sure she is okay?"

Nathan had said little since they first arrived at Laura's house. In fact, he had said little since Mary had clarified that she wanted nothing else to do with him. It's not that he didn't understand. Oh, he understood only too well. He had just hoped, well maybe it was blind hope, but he had hoped that his coming showed that he cared about her. She just didn't seem to care about him. When they find their way to safety, they will part ways; he to Burlington and she, well, whatever. The Hamilton house is no more. But she had made her point clear. There is no us; just her and just me.

Nathan merely nodded once more at Mary's request. He led the way back towards the Secord house. Hopefully, they could stay undetected and be quick about whatever Laura was hoping to find. As they neared the home, Nathan sensed that something wasn't right. The door was ajar, and he could hear noises coming from within. Leaving Laura at the edges of the woods and nearing the door, he looked in. Two American troops were going through the house, pulling and tossing the belongings of the Secords onto the floor.

"We haven't eaten since we've crossed over," the one soldier said. "Find anything to eat?"

"Yeah, here's some bread," he said, tossing it to the other. "Got some cheese and a bit of jerky."

"Give me that. Nothing like a good, home cooked meal. Too bad there aren't some other home-cooked meals if you know what I mean."

Nathan knew exactly what he meant. The women were not safe with such men. They needed to get away. The quicker, the better. As Nathan turned to go, a third American soldier came around the corner.

"Hey, what are you doing snooping around?" The others, still chewing on the jerky, shouted at Nathan. "I should just shoot you on the spot."

"I am an American," Nathan said. "I brought one of the bateau over. Don't you remember me?"

"Maybe we do. Maybe we don't." They leaned in closer to where Nathan stood.

"I was bringing over Colonel Chrystie, but our bateau got caught in the current and taken down river." Nathan was trying to sound convincing, but wasn't sure he could convince himself.

"How come you didn't go back with the Colonel? He went back to Lewiston. Where did you go?"

"I was ordered to stay with the bateau. It had hit a rock and damaged the keel."

"Not much of a sailor if you can't take care of those who do the real fighting," they said, pushing him away and moving on to the next house.

Nathan quickly looked towards where Laura hid. It was no longer safe for her or the others to leave their hiding place. Maybe later, but definitely not now, not with the looks of men like these lurking about. Making certain he wasn't followed, he made his way back to where Laura waited.

"It's too dangerous to go to your house now," he said. "Let's return to the children and wait to see what happens. I don't think it's safe to even try to make our way out of the village. Maybe we should stay hidden for the time being."

As Nathan and Laura were returning to the children, they saw British soldiers coming down the hill towards them. Some were carrying the wounded; others hobbled along, clearly in distress. There were four men, each in a corner, carrying a stretcher with the body of General Brock carefully laid out. On the one corner was one she knew well. Her husband, James Secord, was helping to carry the body of Brock. Behind them was a second stretcher, carrying James McDonnell. Surely this battle has been costlier than the land they fought over.

Chapter 17

Laura Secord quickly moved towards her husband. He didn't see her at first as he tried to keep his footing on the wet hillside. But she saw him, with deep sorrow in his eyes. As their eyes met, there was no need for words. He could see that she was grateful that he was alive and uninjured. She could see the heavy burden upon him, not just because of the loss of General Brock. The invading troops still occupied the high ground. The battle was not yet over.

Major Glegg had the body of General Brock carried to Patrick McCabe's Stone House. Lieutenant-Colonel John Macdonell, critically wounded, was brought to the surgeon at the stone barracks. There wasn't time to mourn, for the battle must still be taken to the enemy. They must be displaced and driven back to Lewiston.

General Sheaffe's troops from Fort George were nearing the heights behind the Americans. They were reinforced with the troops from Fort Chippewa, having run most of the way along Portage Road. Both forts, now under General Sheaffe's command, joined forces for the battle for Queenston Heights

Colonel Scott, of the American army, sought to fortify his position, as his troops murmured against having to fight another battle. Some sought to flee towards the riverbanks and return to Lewiston. A general order went out that the sergeants were to shoot any soldier who left his post without orders. They must stand fast and await the British.

The light company of the 41st moved towards the American lines. They fired a volley and, with bayonets fixed, charged the right flanks of the American troops. The Americans had no weaponry to resist a bayonet attack and fell back in great confusion.

General Sheaffe, seeing the opposing army in disarray, ordered a general attack, pressing his troops towards their enemies. Some immediately surrendered their weapons; others sought to skulk away and disappear in the underbrush. The field gun was quickly taken, and the entire body of American troops was forced back towards the river as the British created a crescent battle line. They now had full control of the flanks.

Those brave enough to run down the hill, pass the redan and towards Queenston, had to face the fire of the troops occupying the lower areas. There was no escape. Colonel Scott, to save the lives of his troops, raised the white flag of surrender as his soldiers laid down their weapons. Thirteen hours after the invasion began, the battle for Queenston Heights was over.

That fateful day, the Americans surrendered to the British one general, six colonels, three majors, seventeen captains and thirty-six subalterns. Yet, for the British, the death of General Brock was an irreplaceable loss.

Chapter 18

Laura Secord, with her five children, had stayed protected in the shadows of the nearby woods as this last battle raged above them. Nathan and Mary, now seated on the ground, pulled the younger children close as their mother stood, eager for any news of her husband.

They had seen the British soldiers press upward towards the heights of Queenston, listened to the sounds of the natives from the woods, and watched as American soldiers sought to find their way through the tree lines to the waters below.

"When do you think it will be safe to move?" Laura asked. "I need to know how James is."

"You can't go out there while the battle still rages," Mary said. "You must think of the safety of the children and of yourself. They need their mother."

"You're right, but it is so hard to just do nothing."

A shout soon echoed down the hill. It was the sound of loud cheering by the British as the white flag of surrender was hoisted by Colonel Scott. The sounds of musket fire near the water's edge soon ceased. Everything, for a moment, became deathly silent.

Laura couldn't wait any longer. Glancing at Mary, she moved from her cover to ascend the hill before her.

"Wait, Laura. I will go with you."

Mary looked back towards the children and Nathan.

"Nathan, will you help us by staying with children? You are still an American and could be arrested or worst, if caught in the open," she asked.

"Go. They will be safe with me."

"Harriett," Laura said. "You are the oldest. I want you to help with the children, but listen to what Nathan says. Stay hidden till I get back."

The two women began the climb upwards towards Queenston Heights.

The British were now leading the captured American troops down the slopes of the hill towards the village of Queenston. Yet not all the American troops had surrendered on that hilltop. Some still lurked in the woods, seeking shelter as they sought how to escape when no one was looking.

The dead and the wounded lay scattered on the hillside as the two women made their way upwards. Each soldier who bore the insignia of the militia was quickly checked by Laura, but still no James.

Nearing the edges of the path, they saw a soldier lying in a heap. He was not wearing the red of the British regulars, but the coat of the Lincoln militia.

There was something familiar about him. Suddenly Laura let out a shriek, seeing her James lying crumpled like a rag doll, as if cast aside by the tragedies of war.

Kneeling by his side, she removed the brush that covered part of his face, the blood still oozing from his battle wounds. His breathing was labored as he lay motionless. Laura reached down and tore off a small piece from the hem of her skirt, making a tourniquet for his wounds. As she tended to the wounds of her husband, three American soldiers, hidden among the trees, emerged from their hiding place. They moved towards her wounded husband, ready to butt him with their muskets.

"Out of the way, woman. You won't need that once we are done with him," they snarled at Laura.

Laura threw her body over her husband, pleading for his life.

"Please, this is my husband, the father of my children. Please do not do this. You can't take his life. We need him. His children need him," she cried.

The one soldier grabbed her by the arm, seeking to toss her aside as the other raised his weapon to club James Secord.

Mary had drawn near, but these soldiers grew ever more menacing. All of their lives were in danger at that moment.

"Please do not do this. Take my life if you must. But save the life of my husband." Her tears streamed down her cheeks as she cried out, but to no avail.

They drew ever nearer to end the life of James Secord, sergeant of the 1st Lincoln militia.

The British troops had continued to lead their captives down the hillside, towards the village of Queenston. The American, Captain Wool heard Laura pleading for the life of her husband..

"Stand down," Captain Wool ordered. "You will surrender your weapons immediately and fall in line with the others."

As these rogue soldiers paused, Laura again laid her body over that of her wounded husband. The British now neared, preparing to fire upon these men. Seeing that they were trapped, they lowered their weapons and surrendered themselves to the conquering forces. Their battle was over.

Laura looked back towards Captain Wool and, with a faint smile, thanked him for saving the life of her husband, but the real battle for his life was still yet to be fought.

Chapter 19

By late afternoon, the battlefield had been cleared of the remaining soldiers. All prisoners had been led down the hillside, past the redan, towards the village of Queenston. The soldiers were ordered to form a line that would lead them towards Fort George. Many looked longingly at the shores from which they had crossed only the previous night. General Van Rensselaer and Colonel Chrystie stood on the heights of Lewiston, watching as their comrades were being led away. The British had won the battle for Queenston Heights; the invasion had been turned back, but with irreplaceable losses on both sides.

Laura had carefully attended to the wounds of her husband as best as she could until help arrived. Four stretcher bearers soon came, lifting James onto the gurney as they began the descent towards Queenston. A makeshift field hospital, near the stone barracks, was overflowing with the wounded. Those most critical being treated first.

James' wounds were very serious. A bullet had grazed his head; another had pierced his arm. His shoulders and one leg showed blood seepage, but the full extent of the wounds would not be known until his clothes were removed. There was no movement by James; his breathing was still labored. The surgeon's assistant assigned James with the severely wounded, to await the surgeon. Laura stayed with him as Mary left to return to the children.

"I will take your children back to your house and stay until you come," she said.

"Thank you," was all Laura could utter, as she stood near the wounded body of her husband.

Nathan and the five children were still huddled within the safety of the woods when Mary arrived. Nathan was seated on the ground, with Charles and Appolonia cradled on his lap. In that moment, all the pent-up emotion let loose as Mary was overwhelmed with tears. Rushing to the children, she sat down, pulling each one close.

"Your daddy is safe, but has been hurt. He is with the surgeon now and your mom is staying with him. We are going to go back to your home until she can come."

Nathan sat quietly as Mary consoled the children and then, thinking his time there was over, he began to move away. Mary grasped his hand, wrapping her fingers around his.

"Please, don't go, at least not yet. I can't thank you enough for saving my life and for helping save the lives of my friends. I am sorry for the way I treated you earlier," she said, wiping her eyes.

Nathan was unsure of what to say or do. Should he just go? After all, he is still an American and with today's events, he will be less welcome in this village. Maybe once everything is over, she will remember why she said what she did and cast him out again. But he knew he could not leave yet. If, for this moment alone, he must do what is right. Letting go of her hand, he reached down and picked up Charles in one arm and Appolonia in the other, as they made their way out of the woods and towards the Secord home.

Chapter 20

War had left its mark on the Secord house, just like many other houses in Queenston. The exterior walls were pitted with the marks of gunfire. The outside orchards had been shredded by grapeshot. Thankfully for the Secord home, though not for those homes closer to the river, it still stood erect and secure. The inside not so much. The ravaging soldiers had torn through whatever they could find. Beds were overturned, pantries emptied, furniture broken. These can be replaced. At least the lives of the children were safe.

Nathan entered the house first to make sure that there were no soldiers hiding within its confines. None was found. Motioning with his hand, the Secord children and Mary made their way to the home. Upon entering, the children began to cry, seeing their house littered with their belongings. This had been an endless day for all of them. Mary wanted to just sit with them and share in their grief, but this was not the moment for doing this.

Making the beds as best she could, the younger children were soon bedded for the night. Mary calmed them by stroking their backs until they fell asleep.

"Your mother will be home soon, you'll see," she said. "For now, we are here to protect you."

Nathan had already cleaned up the main room. Some of the furniture had been broken by the soldiers. Others just tossed aside. He did what he could, but not everything could be saved, not everything could be healed. He paused for a moment, thinking to himself, "What about broken hearts? Can they be healed?"

Surprisingly, the younger children fell quickly asleep as Mary made her way back into the main room. She was surprised at how quickly order had been restored to the Secord home.

"When our cook was taken from us, someone had to keep order in the galley," Nathan said, as if expecting her query. "The Secords have enough on their minds, without having to clean up as well."

Mary said nothing as she leaned against the wall. She too was exhausted, but now was not the time to rest. There was still much to do. She needed to return to the Hamilton estate and see if there was anything left, if it too had been pillaged.

"How long do you plan to be here?" she asked Nathan.

"I don't know. I guess it just depends."

"Depends on what? You do not want to be arrested and sent to Fort George with the others."

"No one really knows that I am here unless you are prepared to have me arrested," he said, finally looking into her face.

Mary, for a moment, blushed but quickly caught herself. Now is not the time for girlish flirting. Besides, they have some unresolved differences between them.

"We could not have done this without you. I will not turn you in, and I know Laura is grateful for your help. Who else really knows that you are here but us?"

"The soldiers who awoke me with their guns in my chest," he offered.

"I will vouch for you and tell them we had business to attend to before the invasion began. They trust me in this village. They will accept my word," she said rather confidently. "Only, well, I have just one more favor to ask. You can say no. If you need to leave, I will understand."

"I can guess, but I think I know what it is already. You want me to stay with the children while you go back to the house," he offered, with little emotion.

"Yes, if you can. If not, then I can stay until Laura returns."

"Go," was all he said.

She wasn't sure whether he was just glad to be free of her; whether he was just annoyed with her or what it was. She gave the older two children a hug as she left, making her way out of the Secord home, not knowing what awaited her.

Chapter 21

Captain Archibald Hamilton was already at the estate of his father when Mary arrived. He had earlier led Holcroft, with his field guns, to these grounds when the British needed to control the waterways. Here they could keep the boats and further reinforcements from crossing the waters of the Niagara.

Mary felt her knees growing weak as she made her way slowly towards the house. This had been a long and exhausting day, but it wasn't fatigue that caused her to feel weak. The house that once stood majestic and tall, overlooking the Niagara River, now lay in a heap of ruins. The grapeshot had pierced ever deeper, shredding the walls with the round shot from the twenty-four pounders. The walls were no more; the upper rooms had fallen into the center. The house had simply collapsed upon itself.

She simply stood there and sobbed deeply as Captain Hamilton drew near and pulled her close. They had always been close, like brother and sister, as she put her head onto his shoulder and wept. The place that they both knew, once filled with laughter and joy was all gone. With it, Mary felt a sense of tremendous loss.

"I did everything in my power to safeguard your home. I tried to keep everything as your father would have wanted it. I just wanted …"

Captain Hamilton took her by the shoulders, lifting her chin.

"Mary, this is not your fault, and no one will ever blame you for what has happened. My father would have been very proud of how you managed his affairs. I am very proud of you. I know you took this job because of a debt your father owed to the estate. I release your family from the debt. You owe us nothing. It is truly we who owe you," he said, with deep tenderness.

"I have to return to my unit," he said. "Do you have anywhere that you can go? Is there any place that you can stay?"

"What about going through the manor? Maybe there is something we can save, something we can find that belonged to your family?" she asked.

"It can wait. It is not safe for you to go into the house, and I don't have the time. Shortly, we will take General Brock and Lieutenant Colonel Macdonell back to Fort George. I don't want you to be alone when we are gone," he said.

"I can stay with the Secords. James was badly wounded, and Laura is with him now. I can help with the children until James comes home."

She watched as Captain Hamilton left, as the 49th prepared for the last journey of General Brock, their beloved leader.

Mary, with one last look at the devastation before her, began her journey through other debris fields, making her way back to the Secord home.

Laura had now returned as Mary entered through the doorway. Nathan was nowhere to be found.

"How is James?" she asked. "Have they finished bandaging him?" hoping that Laura brought good news.

"When I left, the surgeon was still with him. The wounds are very serious. The surgeon told me he will live, but he will carry his wounds for the rest of his life."

Mary pulled Laura tight as they both wept. As if able to read Mary's mind, Laura told her that Nathan had waited for her to return and then quietly slipped out the door. Where he went, she did not know and if he would return, she also didn't know that. She saw the look of disappointment in Mary's eyes, but for the moment, there were more pressing matters. How will the Secord family provide for itself now that their home had been pillaged and their stores emptied? The children still needed to be fed, her husband cared for, and winter was coming.

Chapter 22

A gentle knock sounded at the Secord's home. Laura was busy helping the older children get ready for bed, so Mary moved to answer the door. Pulling the door slightly open, Mary saw Nathan standing in the doorway. Swinging the door wide open, she threw her arms around his neck.

"I thought you had left us. I thought you would never come back."

Nathan didn't know what to say or what to do. His hands were full, but more so, in that moment, his heart was full. Whether this was merely the gratitude of the moment, he didn't know. But it sure felt good to have this blue-eyed, button nose woman hold him tightly.

"Can I come in?" he asked. "I found some food for the family. I hope flour, with cheese and jerky is okay. This should help for a while, at least."

"The soldiers couldn't carry everything away in their haste to escape," he offered. "These were down by that tree near the river's edge."

Laura finally got the children to sleep. Seeing the food Nathan brought, she thanked him for all that he had done for her family that day.

"I don't know what we would have done without you," she said. "You were a godsend to us, and we are so grateful."

"And you, Mary, have been a dear friend for many years. I cannot repay you for all your kindnesses to us." They both teared up once more.

"There's one more thing," Nathan said as he again moved towards the door. "It's the middle of October and the nights are cooler. I took the liberty of also getting some firewood for you. You will need it to keep warm."

He soon returned with an armload of wood, placing it near the fireplace.

"Laura, the estate has been destroyed. There's nothing left but a pile of rubble. Would you be okay if I stayed here tonight until I find other arrangements? I can sleep on the floor over there."

"Absolutely. You are always welcome to stay here," she answered. "Nathan, what about you? What are you going to do? It's getting dark and there is not much light left. Would you consider staying here for the night? Knowing that there was a man in the house would make me feel much safer, at least for tonight."

"I," he stuttered. "I don't know what to say."

"Say yes. All I have is the floor, but I can get some blankets for you," she offered.

"The floor is fine. Laura, if you want to see how James is doing, I will go with you," Nathan said in a quiet voice.

"No. There is not much I can do tonight. The children need me to be here when awake. I will see him in the morning. The surgeon said he would be okay."

Laura brought out some blankets and then, with a smile, found her way to where the children were sleeping. Crawling in beside Charles, she pulled him close and was soon fast asleep.

Nathan had finished stoking the fire as the house bathed in its warmth.

Mary looked at him as if she wanted to say something, but stopped as he put his finger to his lips.

"Mary, we have much to talk about, but not tonight. Neither of us could fully say what's on our hearts and I know you must be so tired. I know I am. Let's find a time tomorrow to talk, if that's okay with you?"

He really didn't give her any chance to answer. Finding their respective places near the warmth of the fire, for this moment, they felt safe from the cannons and musket fires that had so changed their worlds. Mary couldn't help but notice a slight smile on Nathan's lips as she rolled to her side and dropped asleep. Their war for now is over.

Chapter 23

Seasonal changes often came yearly to the people of Queenston. But this morning was different. The frost in the air was more frigid than in previous years. The invasion by the American forces had seen to that.

As the people of Queenston left the security of their homes, at least those who still had homes, the face of their small village changed. The laughter of children, the sound of merchants, the small talk of neighbors were absent as the villagers awoke to their new realities. Their village was now deeply scarred by the ravages of war. Buildings were destroyed and those that still stood showed the scarring of musket fire or cannon shot. It seemed like no one escaped, no one went unscathed by yesterday's events.

The Secord children stirred from their slumber as the morning light broke into their rooms. The older children helped their siblings follow their usual morning routines. Their mother, Laura, had reminded them before they went to sleep of the need to keep order in the home by doing what they always did. But this was not a normal day. Their mother was not in her bed when they awoke. Their father was not in his home. They woke with two strangers who had slept by the fireplace, bringing great uncertainty about what the day would bring.

In the main areas of the small house, the sound of movement was audible. The rattling of pans and the sweet aroma of fresh bread filled their nostrils as they sheepishly looked beyond their rooms to see their mother busy with her chores. Laura greeted each child with a kiss and a hug. At least some things hadn't changed.

Nathan had been up very early, gathering more wood to stoke the fire. He had tried to be silent, not wanting to disturb Mary Johnston as she lay near the fireplace. But truthfully, neither had slept well that night. It wasn't just the hardness of the floor. It wasn't just the harshness of the previous day's war. No, it was much deeper than that. There was something stirring in their hearts, something had awakened itself that Mary had not expected to happen.

Nathan had come to Queenston, hoping to see Mary once more and to help her see the need to escape before the invasion began. Yet as they shared those moments together at the Hamilton estate, she had wanted to know his life's story. He didn't want to tell her because he knew their stories intersected. He knew his grandparents had caused her family great pain. He knew political loyalties had driven her family from the place they called home. And he knew, at least suspected, that if she knew, everything he hoped for would be gone forever. But he told her, and it was as he thought. Or maybe not.

There's a certain power in sharing moments of tragedy that can bring people closer. While it's true that such events can sometimes drive families and friends apart, that wasn't the case here. They had experienced the escape from the estate together. They had aided Laura Secord and her children in finding refuge in the woods near the village. They had faced the day's hardships side by side. As Nathan prepared to depart, as he had initially intended at the estate, she grasped his hand and pleaded for him to stay. Embracing him tightly, she expressed her gratitude in whispers, her warmth thawing the coldness he had previously felt.

But this is a new day. The tragedies of yesterday are over. The Americans had retreated to Lewiston or been taken captive to Fort George. Their common need for survival, which brought them together, was no longer present. Yet his story had not changed. There was nothing he could do about his family's history. There was nothing he could undo. The events of Albany will forever be the same. The only thing he could hope for was that his actions yesterday may yet atone for the sins of his grandparents.

Mary tossed and turned in her makeshift bed, her sleep disturbed by the events of the previous day, her inner turmoil palpable. She had always held a steadfast loyalty to her family's legacy. Despite never having met her grandparents or even her own mother, her father's retelling of the events in Albany was ingrained in her consciousness. Sometimes narrated with fiery indignation, other times with profound sorrow, the tale of their family history echoed through her mind.

Her dad would often say, "If only this hadn't happened. If only they had let us live our lives. Then maybe my mom and dad, maybe my dear wife would still be alive or at least died in peace. I know I have to move on. I know I have to forgive, but the pain is so deep."

Mary had felt her father's pain, and there was little that she could do to console him. And now, here she is, confronted with a man whose family had brought this upon her family. She had made it clear she wanted no more to do with him, never wanting to see him again. But she had not expected this stirring of affection for him. As she sat there, she gave a slight smile to Nathan. Rising, she made her way towards the counter.

Laura had already been up early, firing the kiln, rolling, and kneading the bread. The children needed to be fed first before she left to tend to her husband. At least that's what she kept telling herself. She had seen his wounds and knew the depth of his injuries. She hoped he had made it through the night, pushing away any nagging doubts that may be said differently.

"I need one more favor," Laura asked. "If it's okay to ask?"

"Anything," Mary said. "I promised to help you."

"What do you need?" Mary already knew the answer before it was given.

"I need to see James. I know that you have so much to do. I know you must go back to the estate to clean up. Could you stay here with the children a little longer? I don't want them to see their father yet." Her voice carried almost a plea of desperation.

"Of course, Laura. We will be here until you get back."

Mary had included Nathan in her response, not sure if he would stay but hoping that he might.

Laura again gave her children a hug, told them to mind Mary and quickly left.

Chapter 24

The village of Queenston was not known for its military strength. The main forts were at Fort George and Fort Erie, with soldiers stationed at Chippewa, while others manned field artillery along strategic points overseeing the Niagara River.

But the invasion at Queenston had surprised even General Brock. The village was unprepared and unprotected from the American troops. This unexpected move cost Brock and McDonnell their lives. Yet losing the military leadership of the British forces was great.

Laura Secord, the wife of James Secord, sergeant with the 1st Lincoln militia, made her way down the hillside towards the military barracks. She was grateful that their home was still standing. Some she passed no longer were. Walls had been blown open, furniture scattered, even children's toys were strewn as if a giant hand had simply swept them aside. Looking to her left and up the hill, she paused as she looked at what had once been the proud estate of Robert Hamilton. This towering behemoth of a building was now only a mound of debris. She quickly thought of her dear friend, but for now, she must stay focused on what lay before her. Nearing the barracks, she took a deep breath before entering.

Suddenly, a soldier barred her way.

"What do you want?" he asked. "Why are you here?"

"My husband was wounded yesterday, and they brought him here to the surgeon," she responded quietly. "I have come to see how he is, whether I can take him home with me."

"I am sorry, but you can't enter yet."

General Sheaffe had emerged from the stone barracks, asking the corporal if the preparations were ready.

"Yes, sir, as you ordered. The two wagons will be here shortly, with our best team of horses."

"Good," he said. "I want the 49th to form the honor guard and lead the wagons back to Fort George. The rest can form up behind the two wagons."

"With honor, sir. General Brock was our favorite if you'll pardon me saying so. He came up through the 49th and it is our duty and privilege to serve him one last time." The corporal broke down in tears.

General Sheaffe was to lead the procession, followed by the drummers, the wagons, the pallbearers, and the 49th. The 41st, the Lincoln militias, and other troops were to follow in order as they prepared to follow the route that General Brock had taken the day before.

"Please, all civilians stand aside," the corporal ordered.

Laura moved to the side, along with the others who had gathered for this solemn occasion.

Wooden boxes had been brought to Queenston from Fort George the night before. The bodies were carefully prepared and made ready for their last journey. Honor guards were strategically posted along the route to Fort George.

The horse-drawn munitions wagon stood silently outside of Patrick McCabe's stone house. The honor guard of 49th exited the home and carried the coffin of their fallen officer to the wagon.

A second munitions wagon also stood silently by the barracks. Lieutenant-Colonel McDonnell had been trampled by his falling horse and, after much suffering, succumbed to his injuries. The coffin bearing his body was carefully placed upon this second wagon.

The wagons were now ready, carrying the bodies of these officers who had fallen on the battlefield. The only noise was the occasional neighing of the horses and the marching of soldier's feet. All was as quiet as the occasion itself.

With tenderness, the pallbearers took their place by the coffins, hats and swords carefully adorning the face of each coffin. General Sheaffe made his way to the front of the procession and mounted his horse. The corporal stood at the head of the procession, facing General Sheaffe.

"Attention," he ordered. "Fall in."

The drummers sounded out their funeral dirge as the procession silently moved along the village street.

The sounds of drumming drew the residents of Queenston. Nathan and Mary, rounding up the five Secord children, moved towards the street where the procession was to pass. As the wagons drew near, Mary wept openly for the loss of her friend. General Brock had often dined at the Hamilton estate. She had enjoyed his stories, his tales of great deeds, his character and, most of all, his friendship. This was not just a loss for the British military. This was her loss of a great friend.

Nathan and the children stood beside her. He wanted to reach out and console Mary, but what if, in her loss, she once more rejected him? What if she once more reminded him he was no longer welcomed in Queenston, let alone her life?

As he stood there, he felt a warm and embracing hand slip into his. He did not move. He dared not move, lest the moment be lost. He knew he should mourn, as the others, for those in the funeral procession, but at this moment, he felt a deep sense of joy.

The funeral procession made its way out of Queenston towards Fort George. The people of the village had returned to their homes or what was left of their homes. Yet unseen and unheard by the British soldiers was another army, watching from a distance, a distance spanned by a river of water. But there was no shout of victory. There was no cheering. General Van Rensselaer and Colonel Chrystie stood before their troops, watching the funeral procession. Though enemies by war, they were soldiers and men of honor.

Still bearing the battle wounds of his conflict, General Van Rensselaer raised his arm in salute to these fallen soldiers. Colonel Chrystie and the soldiers of the American forces followed. The brave had fallen, and many other brave men will fall before the conflict is finally over.

Chapter 25

Laura Secord had waited until the coffins were removed and the honor guard had taken its place in the procession. She watched as the procession slowly made its way down the path she had just taken until it was lost from her sight. She had wondered if her children had watched as these brave officers were taken slowly past her home. But for now, she had other things to attend to, her beloved James.

Laura entered the stone barracks. The wounded soldiers were still near the back of the barracks, somewhat crowded in an already cramped space. The room still smelled of death. There is something pungent about drying blood and the smell of gangrene. The mangled limbs of soldiers, removed by the surgeon's blade, were still waiting to be discarded. Laura had braced herself for what she might see, but nothing could prepare her for what sights and smells filled that room.

She saw the attendant that she first met the day before when James was brought in. He was still busy tending to the wounded and assisting the surgeon as he went about his business.

"Sir, excuse me, sir," she said, as she tapped him on the shoulder.

He had been absorbed in his duties and jumped at her touch.

"I am sorry, sir, for startling you. Do you remember me? My husband was brought in yesterday. Secord, James Secord, but I can't seem to see him." Her eyes moving furtively across the wounded.

"Secord, Secord," he said. "Secord of the 1st militia? Let me talk to the surgeon. Stay here."

She had an overwhelming sense of dread settle upon her. Maybe she was too late. Maybe she should have come last night and stayed with him. Her thoughts swirled as the attendant made his way back to her, followed by the surgeon.

"Mrs. Secord?"

"Yes."

"The good news is that your husband is still alive. The bad news is that he has been badly wounded and needs someone to clean his wounds regularly and keep him warm. His body is still in shock. I am afraid that we do not have the room or the people to give him what he needs," he said rather pointedly.

"I am concerned that if he stays here, he will get infected and there is little we can do about that. Or worse still, he will die."

Laura had to fight her continued sense of dread.

"I will care for him. Can he be moved? I will take him home with me."

She had no plan on how she was going to do this or even how the children would respond to their wounded father. She just knew that he could not stay here.

"Do you have someone who could help me? Is there anyone who could help me carry him?" Mary asked.

"I can spare one man to help carry the stretcher, but it will be too heavy for you," the surgeon replied. "If you can find someone to help, I will release him to you."

The surgeon turned away to attend to his duties, leaving Laura alone. Moving towards the doorway, she hurried out as she made her way back towards her house. Her mind was not as much on her children as hoping that this young American, this friend of Mary's, had not left but was still near. He had been a lot of help to her so far. Would he continue to help her?

As she neared her home, she saw the children outside playing near the doorway. Mary was inside, busily cleaning the best she could for her friend.

"Mama," little Apollonia shouted. The rest of the children ran towards her to greet her, but Laura was on a mission. Time was of the essence for her beloved James.

"Is Mary still here?" she asked Charlotte.

"Yes, mama. She's inside cleaning."

Laura called out to Mary, her voice trembling as she spoke. Mary was in the back, thinking the worst, at the sound of her friend's voice.

"Mary, thanks for doing this, but I need Nathan. Is he still here? James is in a bad way, and they can't care for him. I need to bring him home. But do I need someone to help me? He hasn't left, has he?" Laura's voice betrayed her deep sense of anxiety and worry.

"I don't know," Mary said. "He went out and didn't tell me where he was going. I don't know if he has left or is coming back."

"I need to find someone to help. There has to be someone who can help me bring James home."

Mary moved towards her friend. Placing her hand on her shoulder, she drew Laura tight as she whispered to her.

"Laura, we will find someone to help. Let me set up a place for James for when he comes home. What about over there? We can set up his bed and put a curtain around him."

"Yes, whatever you think. The surgeon says that time is of the essence. I need to find someone right now."

Laura rushed through the doorway, almost knocking Nathan over as he drew near with more provisions.

"Nathan, I need your help. Can you help me once more?" Laura pleaded.

"What is it? What do you need?"

"I need to bring James home. They can't tend to him. I am afraid he is going to die. Can you help carry him? The surgeon said that he can provide only one man to help?"

Nathan had to almost run to keep up, as the two quickly made their way back to the stone barracks.

The corporal, standing near the barracks, watched as Laura, with Nathan in tow, neared.

"Stop, what do you want here and what does he want?" the corporal asked, rather menacingly.

"The surgeon said that I can take my husband home. He's here to help me," she said as she tried to brush past him.

"Now, wait a minute. We caught this bloke sleeping near here two days ago. We told you to be on your way." The corporal moved towards Nathan.

The surgeon needed a moment's break, poking his head through the doorway.

"Leave them alone. She is here to get her husband. See that she has some help to get him on a stretcher and carried him out. This will be one less we have to attend to."

"Can't be too careful," the corporal snarled. "With all the goings on around here."

Nathan followed Laura and the corporal through the doorway and to the back area of the barracks. James lay on a table, semi-lucid, as they neared.

Mary gave him a gentle kiss and whispered that they were there to take him home.

James Secord was quickly transferred to the stretcher and, with Nathan on one end and a conscripted soldier on the other, they began their trek back to the Secord's home. The days ahead will be difficult. The time of healing will be slow, but for now, Laura Secord, wife of James, has her beloved husband and her children with her. Together, they can handle anything.

Chapter 26

Mary had prepared an area of the house for James so that when the stretcher came, they could place him carefully on his bed. She had tried her best to make sure that the house was clean, the rooms tidy so that Laura could focus more on caring for her husband, rather than tending to the domestic chores. This was difficult. The outside was still muddy from the previous day's rains. Furniture had been broken by foraging soldiers. But Mary was a gifted organizer, and, with precision, the house was ready for the owners.

The children watched as their father was being carried by two men on a stretcher, Laura leading the way. They said little as the party came through the doorway to the place Mary had prepared. A small table had been placed beside the bed so that the stretcher bearers could more easily transfer him to the bed. Carefully, methodically, and ever so gently, they moved his body from the stretcher to the bed. James offered a few groans of discomfort but shortly, task completed, the soldier folded the stretcher and left.

"Thank you," Mary shouted.

Laura began waiting tenderly for her husband. Now that James was back home, Mary was feeling a need to tend to her own affairs at the Hamilton estate. Laura seemed to sense this.

"I can't thank you enough for what you have done for us," she said. "I could not have done this without your help. I don't know how or if I will ever be able to repay you."

"You have much to do now, Laura," Mary replied.

"Please, go attend to your affairs. My own Mary and Charlotte can help me now. They can fetch water and bring me clean clothes. We'll be okay."

Laura hugged both Mary and Nathan, before returning to her James.

"Go," Laura again said. "We'll be okay."

Mary and Nathan made their way back towards the estate. About halfway, Nathan stopped. Mary sensed he was no longer near.

"We haven't had that talk yet," he said. "Last time we were here, you let it be known that you no longer wanted to see me, ever again. Mary, I'm so sorry for what my family did to your family. If only I could go back and undo everything. Unfortunately, I can't fulfill that wish. I'm sorry, but I'm at a loss for words. If you still want that, I will leave and never come back. I only want you to be happy."

Mary stood quietly for a moment. It was not really a moment of indecision, for she knew what she wanted to do. She had been drawn to this cocky first mate from the Peggy many months ago. He was tall, brawny, and good looking. That hadn't changed. He was still tall, brawny, and good looking, but sure in need of a change of clothes and a bath. She remembered how ridiculous he looked in Mr. Hamilton's clothes and how uncomfortable he felt. But then she looked down at her own dress, dirty and tattered in places, thinking that she was no catch of the day either.

Mary gently put her arms around his neck and pulled him close. Nathan didn't need instructions about what to do next. He pulled her tight in a warm embrace.

"No, we can't go back and undo what has happened. We can only move forward," she said. "I forgive your family for what they did. I don't know what my dad will say, but we'll take it when it comes."

As Nathan and Mary's tender embrace lingered, their hearts spoke volumes in the silent language of love. In that fleeting moment, amidst the chaos of war and destruction, they found solace in each other's arms, their affection blooming like a fragile flower amidst the rubble of the Hamilton estate.

Surveying the surrounding devastation, Nathan's gaze shifted from Mary's mesmerizing eyes to the ruins of the once-majestic Hamilton estate. Where there was once grandeur and splendor, now lay only desolation and ruin. The relentless barrage of artillery fire had reduced the estate to nothing but a heap of rubble, its walls torn asunder by the merciless onslaught of cannon fire. As the echoes of destruction faded, all that remained was a haunting silence, punctuated only by the echoes of their shared embrace.

Mary stood there with her hand in Nathan's, not knowing what to do or where to begin. There were no doors to go through. Just rubble to climb over.

"I met Captain Hamilton here yesterday," she finally said. "He told me that there was nothing that I could have done, but I feel so helpless. They had entrusted the care of the home to me. Maybe if I have stayed, they would have spared the home."

"If you had stayed, you would have been under that pile of rubble. Captain Hamilton is right. You could not have saved the home. You barely escaped with your life."

"If you had not come, I would have been buried under that pile," she said, squeezing his hand tighter.

"Captain Hamilton also told me that the debt my father owed the estate was forgiven. My dad is now free." The pent-up emotion broke forth in loud, sobbing tears.

Nathan said little as he pulled her close. Life for both of them has changed, their futures uncertain but with a difference. They now had each other, and, for the moment, that is sufficient.

Chapter 27

The funeral procession had snaked its way along the roadway that led towards Fort George. Passing by Voorman's Point, the soldiers had left their posts to line the route, standing erect and saluting as the bodies of Brock and McDonnell passed by. The route had several small homesteads dotted throughout. Even as far away as St. Davids, the people came and lined the roadway in silence as the drummers continued their slow, methodical beat.

By mid-afternoon, the procession neared Fort George. Two days earlier, the guns of Fort Niagara had fired their salvo across the Niagara River, only to be echoed in response by the guns of Fort George. This day, General Van Rensselaer had ordered that the guns of Fort Niagara were to remain silent as the British prepared to bury their dead.

The procession continued past Fort George until it reached the Government House in Niagara. The streets were crowded, each standing silent as the wagons, with their beloved leaders, pulled up in front of the building. Standing on the stairs, leading to the building, stood Major Glegg.

The corporal, at the head of the procession, turned to face the party as the drummers continued to beat their funeral dirge.

"Attention," he ordered.

The drummers, with one last beat, went silent as the air became still with the solemnity of the occasion.

A private of the 49th drew near to General Sheaffe. The General dismounted as the private held the harness of this majestic steed.

"Pallbearers, take your place," the corporal continued. "Honor guard, fall in."

The honor guard of the 49th lined both sides of the steps into the building as the pallbearers took their place behind the wagons bearing the coffins.

A muscular sergeant gently began pulling the handle bearing Brock's coffin toward the rear of the wagon. The pallbearers lifted the coffin and, with precision, placed it upon their shoulders.

Arriving at the base of the stairs, they waited until those bearing the coffin of MacDonnell took their place behind his beloved general.

General Sheaffe made his way up the stairs, where he stood with Major Glegg and Rev. Addison, the presiding Anglican clergyman.

The corporal again took his place by the stairs.

"Pallbearers," he shouted, "Proceed."

The sounds of the drummers once more sounded their mournful beat, the pallbearers making their way up the stairs. The honor guard stood at attention, each saluting their fallen officers. Entering through the doorway, they made their way to the room where the bodies were to lie in state.

The honor guard, in shifts of two hours, was assigned to stand guard around the caskets. Others took their place by the doorway into the Government House.

As the dust settled from the recent battle at Queenston Heights, both the British and the Americans found themselves in a state of uncertainty. While the British remained vigilant, unsure of whether another American offensive loomed on the horizon, General Van Rensselaer had opted to halt his troops' advance. Recognizing the need to reassess their strategies, they regrouped to plan their next move before launching any further attempts to breach Canadian territory.

Meanwhile, Nathan and Mary made their way back to the Secord homestead, their hearts heavy with the weight of recent events. With the Hamilton estate reduced to rubble, their focus shifted to the practical task of salvaging what they could from the debris. Mary understood the importance of hiring a crew to aid in the cleanup efforts, knowing that it was the first step toward rebuilding what had been lost. As they contemplated the future of the Hamilton family's estate, they resolved to face the challenges ahead with resilience and determination.

The younger children saw them coming up the road before they even reached the homestead.

"Mary," they shouted, running towards her. "You've come back to us."

Charlotte, the oldest of the four, with Appolonia firmly held in her arms, arrived first. Mary kneeled before them, as the children threw themselves into her arms.

"I am so glad to see you," Charlotte asked. "Can you stay with us?"

"Only for a few moments," Mary said. By this time, Harriett had arrived, with Charles in tow.

As Mary reached out to pull Charles tight, he moved away and tugged at the pants of Nathan.

"It seems like he would rather have you than me," Mary laughed. Nathan lifted Charles high in the air and pulled him tight.

"I am so glad to see you." Charles had thrown his arms around Nathan's neck and hung on.

"Where's your sister, Mary?" Nathan asked.

"She's helping mother with father, getting the water and helping to make the meals."

Mary brushed the face of the children as she rose and moved towards the Secord home. Gently pushing the door open, she saw Laura attending to James. She looked tired and worn, but greeted them warmly as they came into the room.

"Mary," Laura said. "I am so glad to see you. How are you? How are things at the estate?"

"Laura, my good friend. There is much to do but little that we can do now. It must wait. How are you? How is James?" Mary glanced at where he lay, on the bed she had made for him.

"He is restless and has a fever. I am trying to keep his wounds bathed and changed. I am doing the best I can. Mary here has been a great help to me," she said, as she put her arm around her eldest daughter.

As to not forget the rest, she added, "And where would I be without the help of Charlotte and Harriett and Charles and even Appolonia?"

"The surgeon dropped in early this morning," she added, "to make sure that everything is okay. He said it is a waiting game, that there is little we can do until the fever breaks and the swelling goes down. Then we will know for certain. But Mary, have hope because James squeezed my hand ever so gently this morning."

"Is there anything that we can do for you?" Mary asked. "I need to see how my father is doing."

"No, there isn't much that anyone can do right now. The village is still on edge, wondering when the next invasion will happen. What things we can still find in the garden we have brought inside. But because James was in the militia, the soldiers have assured me they will help us with provisions. We will be okay. You go to your father."

They heard a loud banging behind them.

"Sorry," Nathan said as he piled more wood near the fireplace. "I thought you may need this before the night settles in. It looks like it is going to be a frosty night."

"Thanks," Laura said. With a last hug, she turned back to attend to her beloved James.

Mary and Nathan bade each of the children farewell and left the Secord home, to walk the path that would lead them to St. Davids and the home of Mary's father, George Johnson. Both were quiet as they walked along, unsure of how Mary's father would respond to this tall, good-looking sailor who had captured the heart of his daughter but who bore the name Douglas.

Chapter 28

Mary and Nathan arrived at the Johnson home later in the afternoon. The roads had dried, making them easier to walk along. By late afternoon, the sun was dipping in the western skies as the night air showed the signs of the season they were now entering. Both pulled their cloaks tighter around their neck as they drew closer to the homestead.

Suddenly, Nathan stopped. Mary was absorbed in her own thoughts and continued to walk on until she sensed he was not at her side. She saw Nathan looking beyond her to the homestead.

"What's wrong?" Mary asked. "Why have you stopped?"

"I don't know if I can do this," he said. "I don't know how your father will react to me, how he will react towards you if I continue. Maybe it's better for both of us if I don't go to his house."

"You can't stop now," she said. "We're almost there. You don't know what he'll say or what he'll do."

"I know how you reacted at the Hamilton estate," he said. "You wanted nothing more to do with me."

"Yes, but that was before everything happened. It was you who saved my life. Going back is not possible. You can't undo what your grandfather did. Let's take it slowly."

She walked back to him. Taking his hand, she gently pulled him as she turned to continue the journey to her father's home, the home she had known as a young lady.

Nathan continued to hold her hand as they walked toward the homestead. Both seemed to walk slower as they came to the lane that would lead them to the house.

George Johnson had never remarried after Mary's mother died. It had been difficult managing the farm and raising a young daughter, but he felt he could never find anyone like his beloved Rebecca. They had been childhood sweethearts in Albany. It just didn't seem right to share his life with another.

As they entered the lane and began the not-so-long walk, the sun was setting. While the house remained dark, Mary was confident that her father would be finishing his chores around the back corner. The cows still needed to be milked and fed. The eggs needed to be gathered, and the chickens settled back into their coop for the night.

Mary smiled as she thought back to the many hours she had helped her father.

Nearing the house, she saw her father rounding the corner as he moved towards the front door. His head was down, his shoulders stooped, but his walk was unmistakable. He always had a determined stride, always seemed to walk with purpose. As she watched him moving towards them, she had a flashback as she saw herself running as a child, trying to keep up. It had been some time since she had been home to visit her father. It just felt good to be here.

Startled, George Johnson straightened up as he stared off, trying to gain some recognition of who or what was near his house. These were unsettled times, and he knew the Americans had been defeated at Queenston, but that was a few days ago. Maybe they had returned. As if returning from a daydream, he smiled.

"Mary, Mary, is that you? Have you come?"

"Yes, papa, it is I," she said as she ran towards him, throwing her arms around his neck. "I have come home to see you. Are you alright? Are you okay?"

"Yes, yes," he answered. "You must come in. You never know …" Suddenly, he saw another standing off to the side, watching as this unfolded before him.

Even before her father could ask, Mary offered it up to him.

"Papa, this is Nathan. He has come with me from Queenston. He is a friend. If it is okay, can he come in, papa?" she asked, searching his eyes for an answer.

"If he is your friend, yes, yes, he can come in." George Johnson pushed open the door and entered, Mary and Nathan following.

The homestead was very simple in appearance, not quite like the Secord home. It was more like a bachelor's home, a place where a man may live, but lacking the charm that only a woman can bring. But it was his home. George moved towards the fireplace, stoking the embers, and setting in new logs. It wasn't long before the fire glowed, bringing both light and warmth to the small home.

Mary lit some candles and moved towards the pantry. She knew this area well, for this had been her domain for so many years. She placed a loaf of bread under her one arm and gathered up some cheese and smoked sausage that her father had made with the other. Every year, while she was growing up, they would buy a piglet from another farmer, raise it to maturity and use it to supply fresh meat during the winter months. Her father made the best sausage in the entire area. At least that was what Mary always believed and told everyone who had an ear to listen.

The food was placed on the table, the chairs pulled up as the three of them sat down. Her father couldn't seem to take his eyes off of his daughter.

"Mary, I heard that the Hamilton estate had been blown up. I asked around, but no one seemed to know what had happened to you. Were you there when it happened? How did you escape the invasion?" he asked. He still had touched none of the food before him.

"Papa, it was bad, really bad. The Americans started blowing up the village in the middle of the night. I, we barely escaped from there with our lives," she said.

George glanced over at Nathan, who sat somewhat with his head down, waiting for Mr. Johnson to ask him to leave, but he said nothing.

"Papa, it's not what you may think. Nathan is a sailor who brought supplies for the Hamilton estate last May. He heard the army was going to invade. He came to warn me. I needed to leave. I would have died when the house was destroyed if Nathan had not come. She reached over to squeeze Nathan's hand and said, 'Papa, he saved my life'."

"Papa, he is my friend. He also has nowhere else to go. Please, may he stay here tonight?" Mary asked, as she reached across, taking her father's callous hand in hers.

"Let's eat," was all that was said.

He broke off some bread, stacked it with cheese and sausage, and attacked his food with vigor. Nathan sat and watched, unsure of whether to stay or get up and go. "Eat," George said, pushing the meal towards Nathan.

Mary's smile lingered as she observed Nathan breaking off a piece of bread and joining her father in their shared mealtime routine. The comfort of eating together, especially in the familiar surroundings of her childhood home, brought a sense of warmth and solace. For now, she decided, they would simply relish this moment of respite, setting aside the weightier matters that await discussion. There would be time for Nathan to share his story later.

As Nathan reclined by the fireplace, enveloped in the soft glow of its fading embers, his mind remained restless, resisting the embrace of sleep. The rhythmic cadence of George and Mary's breathing provided a soothing backdrop, a reminder of the safety and sanctuary he had helped secure for Mary. Despite his own restlessness, witnessing their peaceful slumber brought a measure of contentment to Nathan's troubled soul. In the night's quiet, he could only hope that Mary's feelings toward him remained unchanged as the dawn approached.

The rooster crowed early in the morning, signaling that it was time to rise and get about the morning chores. Nathan had drifted in and out of sleep but was awakened both by the rooster and the smell of brewing coffee.

"It's about time you got up," Mary said with a smile. "I trust you slept well."

Nathan stretched the stiffness out of his back as he sat up. Trying to rise, he stumbled a bit as he sought to regain a sense of balance.

"Yes, thank you for the bed," he said. "Where's your father?"

"He's already gone to milk the cows. We only have two cows, but they are good milkers. They have given us all that we could use. Sometimes papa will share the extra with the neighbors. He always felt that it was important to share with others. He learned that from his father in Albany," she said.

Mary gathered together some of what they had for supper the previous evening.

"We don't have a lot of variety," she said, "but the food is always fresh. Can I get you some coffee? Papa will be in soon."

"Please, thank you. Mary, did you talk with your father after I went to bed last night? Did you talk about the invasion or what happened?" he asked.

"Really, what you want to know is if we talked about you, don't you?" she replied.

Nathan stood there with a sheepish smile. She was right.

"No. That must wait. We talked about going to General Brock's funeral today. I need to be there. He was my friend and I need to pay my respects," she said, as she teared up.

"Papa has promised to take me to Niagara when the chores are done. He got up earlier than usual to do this so we could be there in time. We need to be there by ten. Will you come with us?"

"I don't know. Should I?" he asked.

"I want you to come, but I will not pressure you to do so. You have done so much for me already. Whatever you decide, I will accept."

Nathan wanted to go, wanted to be with her. He was not so sure about being with her father. The ride to Niagara will take at least two hours, that's two hours each way in which her father can ask all kinds of questions, questions that he is not so sure that he wants to answer. But he wants to be with Mary. She will mourn the loss of her friend and he wants to be at her side for this. Besides, what would he do if he stayed here by himself? The questions, answers, and uncertainties continued to swirl around Nathan's head as George Johnson walked through the door.

"Chores are done for now," he said. "The rest can wait till we get home. The wagon is ready when you are. Let me get a quick bite to eat and get cleaned up."

George looked at Nathan. "You coming with us? Hate to say it, but best if you get cleaned up a bit. Those are fine folk in Newark. They don't take to us homesteaders too much. They say we smell like the farm, as if their perfumes don't stink," he said with a chuckle.

Chapter 29

The ride to Newark was not quite what Nathan had been expecting. He had created this total scene in his mind of how it would be and what would be the outcome of his own story. It told different from what he thought would happen.

The wagon wasn't very large but big enough to be pulled by one horse, and not large enough to need more. George used it mostly for bringing in the hay from the fields or if he needed to take some produce or meat to the Secord store to be sold among the people at Queenston. Sometimes, he would load up his wagon to take milk and food to a widow with five children. Other times he would take a sick neighbor to Queenston or Newark to see the doctor. He believed it is important to help others because you never know when you will need help.

There was a bench seat up front. George sat on the left, gathering the reins in his hands. Motioning to Mary to sit beside him, she climbed up. George wasn't really trying to ignore Nathan, but there was so much to catch up on with his daughter. Since the harvest had been gathered and the supplies were ready for the coming winter, there wasn't a need to go into Queenston, but how he missed seeing her.

Nathan climbed onto the back, with feet dangling over the edges. The road had become rutted from the recent storms, some places more deeply than others, but the horse seemed to have a sense of what ruts to avoid. When it wasn't possible, the horse would slow down and bring the wagon gently over the ruts.

"Took me a long time to teach this horse how to miss those ruts," George shouted back to Nathan with a broad smile.

Nathan relaxed somewhat, at least as much as he could, as they moved ever closer to the town of Newark.

Newark had once been the capital of Upper Canada under Governor Simcoe. The Government Building, which for the moment housed the bodies of General Brock and Lieutenant Colonel MacDonell, had held parliament until it moved to York. Today the building bustled with the military as they prepared to lay to rest their beloved officers.

The Johnson wagon tried to move down King Street and find a place closer to Queen Street, but it was not possible. Many others were of the same mind, having the same desire to be here and pay their respects to these fallen comrades. George pulled the wagon onto a small side street, wrapped the reins around a post and began their walk towards Queen Street.

"Mary, Mary, is that you?" A voice came from the crowd.

Looking around to see who might call her name, she saw Captain Archibald Hamilton waving at her through the crowd.

"Mary, over here. Come over here," he said, as he shouted over the noise of the crowd.

Mary squeezed her way through the jostling crowd, careful to wait for her father and Nathan, as they followed her to where Hamilton stood.

"Mary, it's so good to see you." I am so glad that you can come. General Brock, may he rest in peace, would be so proud of you being here to honor him.

Captain Hamilton was dressed in his bright red vest and black epaulets, looking ever like the military officer and gentleman that he was.

"Is this your father?" he asked.

"Yes, this is my papa," Mary said, as she placed her arm into the crook of her father's arm.

"This also is Nathan," she added. "He saved my life just before the estate was destroyed."

Captain Hamilton reached out and shook the hand of both George and Nathan.

"So good to meet you. I wish it was under different circumstances, but maybe later," he said.

Captain Hamilton turned back to Mary.

"Have you talked with your father about what we spoke about?" he asked. "All my siblings agree with that decision."

A sound of a bugle could be heard in the background as the troops were being called to assemble for the solemn procession that lay before them.

As Hamilton bade his farewell and departed, Mary and her father were left with a lingering sense of gratitude and curiosity. George's expression betrayed a hint of puzzlement at the unexpected encounter. Mary, sensing her father's unspoken question, reassured him with a gentle promise of explanation to come.

"Later, papa," she assured him, her words carrying the weight of unspoken thoughts. "I will tell you later."

In the quiet aftermath of Hamilton's departure, Mary's mind drifted to the recent events and the complexities they introduced into their lives. However, before she could dwell further on the matter, her thoughts were interrupted by a new development that unfolded with the news of General Sheaffe's outreach following Brock's demise.

Fort. George, 16th Oct.1812.

Sir – I have heard with deep regret that Col. Van Rensselaer is badly wounded. If there be anything in my command, that your side of the river cannot furnish, which would be either useful or agreeable to him, I beg that you will be so good as to have me apprised of it. I have the honor to be, sir, with much esteem.

Your very devoted servant,
R.U. Sheaffe.

*****

Sheaffe wrote a further letter to Van Rensselaer.

Sir – As the period assigned to the cessation of hostilities is drawing to a termination; and the intended exchange of prisoners and sending over the wounded and the militia will require much more time than remains of it; and as, moreover, part of this day is to be devoted to paying the last offices of humanity to the remains of my departed friend and General, I feel it to be my duty to propose a prolongation of the armistice to such a period as may be necessary for the complete execution of those humane purposes. Lists are prepared for all the prisoners here, distinguishing those of the line from militia; and Brigadier-Major Evans, who has been appointed by me to arrange the business with Capt. Dox will be ready to proceed in it as soon as that officers comes over. I have the honor.

*****

General van Rensselaer sent his response.
Headquarters, Lewiston, Oct. 16th 1812.

Sir – I have this moment had the honour to receive your two letters of the present date. I most cheerfully agree to extend the cessation of hostilities for a time amply sufficient to discharge all duties of humanity to the brave who are wounded, or prisoners; and the just tribute of respect to the gallant dead. For these purposes, I agree to the further cessation of hostilities, until 4 o'clock of the afternoon of the 19th instant.

I shall order a salute for the funeral of General Brock to be fired here, and at Fort Niagara, this afternoon.

You will please to accept, sir the grateful acknowledgements of Col. Van Rensselaer and myself, for your kind offer of anything in your power which might contribute to his comfort. I do not know that he is at present destitute of anything essential.

As this, sir, is probably the last communication I shall have the honor to make to you from this station, I avail myself of the opportunity to tender you the assurance of my great esteem and consideration.

Captain Leonard of Fort Niagara acknowledged the communique from General van Rensselaer, that the salute to Gen. Brock would be fired at sunset.

*****

A last letter was sent from General Sheaffe to General Van Rensselaer from Fort George on the day of Brock's funeral.

Sir – I feel too strongly the generous tribute which you propose to pay to my departed friend and chief, to be able to express the sense I entertain of it. Noble minded as he was, so would he have done himself. I have directed the prolongation of the armistice until four o'clock in the afternoon of the 19th instant, to be communicated along this line.

*****

The streets in Newark were crowded with people from different places, both locally and farther away. General Brock had been respected by many as a capable leader. His death was felt by all.

The troops had formed up, with reverse arms across from Government House as all flags flew at half-mast. Along the streets, people sought the best places, even jostling with others. The procession was scheduled to begin at 10 am., beginning at the Government House on Queen Street. At King Street, Queen Street's name changed to Picton Street. It was just a continuation of the route that would take them to Fort George and the burial places for Brock and MacDonell.

By 9:50, the funeral participants were in place. It was to be led by Major Campbell, followed by sixty men of the 41st Regiment, led by a subaltern. Sixty members of the militia, led by a captain, were to follow, with two six-pounder guns firing every minute. The Band of the 41st and the remaining detachments from the Fort were next in line. Though not in the procession, over 200 natives formed a line two deep along the route that the procession was to take.

The Regimental Band of the 41st, with their drums covered with black cloth, were to follow next, followed by General Brock's horse, Alfred, being fully covered with rich, decorative coverings and tended to by four groomsmen. Each of the military surgeons and Brock's servants took their place in line.

By 10 am, the streets of Newark were silent. There was no talking, no shouting, no laughter. Even the children were as silent as the occasion demanded.

The corporal of the 49th ascended the stairs and called the procession to order.

"Attention," he commanded, as Rev. Addison appeared in the doorway of the Government House. It was now time to pay tribute to these fallen officers. In silence, the soldiers and militia stood. From the House, the first casket carrying the remains of Lieutenant Colonel MacDonnell was brought forth. The pallbearers walked behind Rev. Addison down the stairs as he stood at the foot of the wagon. With a sword and hat adorning the wooden face, the casket was carefully placed on the wagon. The wagon was moved forward as the second wagon was moved to the base of the stairs.

In the doorway of the Government House, the pallbearers carrying General Brock's casket came into view. With military precision, the pallbearers passed through the honor guard, still lining the sides of the stairway, as they saluted their General. Making their way down the stairs, they took their place at the rear of the wagon and gently placed Brock's body in its center, hat and sword on top. Rev. Addison stood quietly by its side until all was in place.

The corporal still stood on the steps of the Government House.

"Attention. Fall in."

The band of the 41st Regiment played Handel's Dead March.

Stoic, seasoned military men wept silently in their mourning. Sobs were heard coming from the crowds lining the streets. The natives, standing in their finest, were led by their fearless leader, Tecumseh, the friend of Brock. Even sounds across the river could be heard, sounds of the minute guns coming from Fort Niagara, as Colonel Winifred Scott later wrote, "as a mark of respect to a brave enemy".

The funeral procession passed through the gates of Fort George as the wagons were brought near the north-east cavalier bastion. One grave had been dug in the bastion that would hold the bodies of both soldiers, who fought as one in life, who were interred as one in death.

Rev. Addison read from the Church of England Book of Common Prayer, the ceremony for the dead, as those of high rank and common foot soldier stood in silence. With the final amen, the two bodies were lowered into the ground. With one final salute, they honored their fallen comrades.

Major Glegg, Brock's Aid-de-camp and the one who gave oversight to the funeral arrangements and service, stood in the open air. In his hand was a piece of paper. He looked at the other officers and privates, men who had served their General well.

"I am not much for poetry," he said, "But let me end this day with the following tribute to our fallen General, remembering his great triumph at Fort Detroit."

"Thou, sixteenth of August, shall raise admiration
And oft be productive of proud emu'ation,
The Troops and Militia stood firm as a rock
Who fears thrice the number when marshall'd by BROCK?
To capture an army that counts three to one
A fortress and state, hardly losing a man,
Will long be remember'd a capital stroke
And quoted uniquely, 'The glory of Brock."

*****

"Long live his memory. Long live the King." Major Glegg turned and nodded to the corporal, who, with a loud voice, shouted, "Party dismissed." The ceremony that marked the funerals of General Brock and Lieutenant Colonel MacDonnell had now ended.

The grave diggers completed their task, the bastion sealed, and the funeral party returned to their respective posts.

At 4 pm, General van Rensselaer ordered from Lewiston a twenty-one-gun salute.

Yet the Declaration of War by James Madison has not been rescinded. The war had not ended with the American defeat at Queenston. There were to be more dark days ahead for the people of Niagara.

Chapter 30

Mary had wanted to join in the funeral procession as the larger crowd of personal mourners walked behind. Maybe if she was by herself, she may have, but today she was with her father and her friend. She couldn't stay long. George needed to get back to the farm. The chores would wait for his return, but the cows still needed to be milked. As for her and Nathan, well, she just did not know what to think. The past few days have been a whirlwind, completely changing the direction of her life. Once thinking that her future was secure and ordered, all now has changed. Mary preferred predictability, not uncertainty. She needed order and security but now her life had been tossed into disorder, with seemingly no clear path before her.

The crowds soon dispersed. Shops were reopened, as store clerks attended to those homesteaders' needing supplies for the coming days. But George was well-prepared for the coming winter months. His stores were full; his hay carefully stacked; his provisions ready.

The three travelers made their way back to where they had left their horse and wagon. Nothing had changed from the moment they had tied up the horse. George put his arm around its neck, gently stroking its side. Pulling an apple from his pocket for such an occasion, he placed it in his palm as the horse gladly took this treat from him.

"Ah, Becky," he said. "You have always been good to me."

Unhitching the Becky, he again sat on the left as Mary climbed up beside him. Nathan stood near the back, with his hand on the wagon's side, not yet having climbed up.

"What are you waiting for?" George said. "Aren't you coming back with us? Come on, get in." He gave a quick flip of the reins as Becky began her circle back to King Street and towards home.

Mary wanted to get out of the wagon and grab Nathan, to urge him to come with them. But this had to be his decision. Either he wanted to be with her, or he didn't. He must decide. She can't decide for him. She sat with her father, face forward as the wagon continued to inch away from Nathan.

With a deep sigh, Nathan quickly ran and jumped onto the back. Mary smiled as she felt the change in weight on the wagon. He made the right decision, at least for her.

As they left Newark towards St. Davids, George was deeply absorbed in his own thoughts. He wanted to know more about this man that Mary had brought home with her. After all, he was her father, and you would think that he would have a right to know more about him. George saw how Mary looked at Nathan and he at her. They tried to be coy about it, but George wasn't that old that he forgot what those little furtive glances meant.

Another thought came back to him. What did Captain Hamilton mean when he asked Mary if she had told him yet? Told him what? George had business dealings with the Hamilton estate before, and that hadn't gone too well. He was on the verge of losing everything that he had worked for when suddenly he was told that he could keep the farm and work it like he had always done so. They even offered Mary a job.. Why? He didn't know. All he knew was that after his little girl, after his grown daughter had left, the home seemed empty and lonely.

"Mary," he said. "I'm so sorry for what happened to the Hamilton estate, but you don't know how glad I am to see you." He reached out and gave her hand a squeeze.

"I know you will talk about what happened when you are ready. I won't ask you anything if you don't want me to."

Fathers have this way with their daughters that can get them to talk, even when they don't want to say anything.

Mary had been silent for a reason. She knew they needed to have this conversation about Nathan. She wanted her father to like Nathan, to accept him into the family, to not reject him, but she knew that there had been so much hurt brought by her father from Albany. This was not a conversation that she wanted to have but have it they must, though maybe not today.

She knew she needed to talk to him about the Hamilton Estate, about what Captain Hamilton meant when he asked her if she had spoken to her father yet. She had kept the details of why she went to work for the Hamilton's from him. Her father was such a proud man. He would have given up the farm before he would put his daughter in such a difficult position. It had been easier to just not let him know. But not now. He needed to know.

Mary went back and forth in her mind. Should we talk about Nathan, or should we talk about the Hamilton's? Finally, she decided that the Hamilton's only involved her and might be the easier of the two, if that was at all possible.

"Papa," she said. "You know I love you and that I would do anything for you." She reached across and squeezed his hand. He said nothing. Mary wiggled a bit as she continued to summon her nerve to bring up finally what she had kept hidden from him.

"Papa, do you remember when the crops failed and times got really hard for the farm, for you and me at the farm?"

"How could I forget?" he said. "It was all we could do to survive. Little food for ourselves. Little food for our animals. It couldn't get any darker, unless maybe when your mama died."

"Yes, papa. I remember you walking the fields, sitting at the table with your head in your hands. I so wanted to help, but there wasn't much I could do," Mary said.

"There wasn't much any of us could do. The weather was against us, that's all."

"Papa, you remember when I came to you and told you that the Hamilton estate lent out money to people just like us, homesteaders having a tough time? We thought that if we could just get enough to get by, then we could repay it back with next year's crops."

"Yes," he said. "But next year's crops failed and the year after was not much better. I met with the Hamilton's, begging them to give us more time to repay, but they said it had already been too long. They wanted our farm, the farm that my parents had helped build, the farm that your mother had lived and died on, the farm where I raised you. They wanted to take it all away from us and there was nothing I could do to stop them."

"I know, papa," Mary whispered.

"But then," George said, "I got this letter from them telling me I can stay on the farm and work out something with them for repayment. I don't understand why they did this. The Hamilton's were always shrewd in their business dealings. They didn't give little guys like me a break."

Nathan listened as Mary struggled to tell her father what truly happened. He knew. He knew the sacrifices that they all had made so that they could keep the farm.

They rode about another mile in silence, when Mary blurted out, "Papa, I have something to tell you. Please don't get mad at me, papa. I did this for us. I did this for you."

He looked at her as the reins drooped in his hands.

"Papa, you never knew why I left home to work for the Hamilton's. It was the hardest thing that I had to do, but I did it for us, for you."

George stiffened a little on the bench but said nothing.

"Papa, they said that if I worked for them, they would allow the farm to stay in the family. They said that I could work off what we owed if I oversee the estate for them. Papa, please don't be mad. I did this for us." The tears now flowed freely down Mary's cheeks, as she suddenly went silent.

George honestly didn't know what to say, whether to be angry, joyful, sad, mad or what. Meanwhile, he remained seated, staring straight ahead. Being angry with the Hamilton's was out of the question, and being angry with his daughter was definitely not an option. He had borrowed the money to keep the farm afloat. He made that decision. No one forced him to have this lien placed against his farm.

"What did Captain Hamilton think you should tell me?" George asked.

"Papa, the estate is no more. There is nothing for me to go back to. The Hamilton family has agreed, because of my service to them, that our debt is repaid and that what we owe is forgiven. Papa, we don't owe them any more money."

George said nothing more. The trip home was quiet as each pondered what this meant. Yet for Mary, though this was hard, it was the easiest of the two. The hardest was yet to come, and she wasn't sure that she was ready for that.

Chapter 31

General Brock had been both the commander of the troops in the Upper Province and the administrator of the Civil Government. With his death, General Sheaffe, the ranking British officer, was now appointed by George Prevost as Lieutenant General and the colonial administrator.

General Sheaffe, like his predecessor, was both a professional soldier and an honorable man. He was quick to draft a letter to Prevost outlining the events of the Battle for Queenston Heights. With his tale of the events, he gave quick praise to each of the commanding officers as they had led their troops to victory.

"Captain Dennis and Williams, commanding the flank companies of the 49th Regiment, which were stationed at Queenston, were wounded, bravely contending at the head of their men, against superior numbers; but I am glad to have it in my power to add that Capt. Dennis, fortunately, could keep the field, though with great pain and difficulty, and Capt. William's wound is not likely to deprive me long of his services.

I am indebted to Capt. Holcroft of the Royal Artillery, for his judicious co-operation with the guns and howitzers under his immediate superintendence, the well-directed fire which contributed materially to the fortunate result of the day.

Capt. Derenzy, of the 41st reg. brought up the reinforcements of that corps from Fort George and Capt. Bullock led that of the same regiment from Chippawa; and under their command, those detachments acquitted themselves in such a manner as to sustain the reputation which the 41st Regiment had already gained in the vicinity.

Major-gen Brock, soon after his arrival at Queenston had sent down orders for battering the American Fort Niagara: Brigadier-major Evans, who was left in charge of the operations against it with so much effect, as to silence its fire, and to force the troops to abandon it, and his prudent precautions he prevented mischief of a most serious nature, which otherwise might have been effected, the Enemy have used heated shot in firing at Fort George. In these services, he was effectually aided by Col. Claus (who remained in the fort at my desire) and by Capt. Vigoreux of the Royal Engineers.
Brigadier-major Evans also mentions the conduct of Capts. Powell and Cameron, of the militia artillery, in terms of commendation…"

The cessation of hostilities between the two countries was only to last three days until the 19th of October. With the burial of the dead, both officers and regulars, it was soon time to prepare for another invasion by the American forces.

General Sheaffe issued a general order that the forts, George, and Erie, were to be fortified and that sentries were to be doubled and troops stationed at any other points of possible invasion, such as Queenston. The invasion on the 13th had taken the British forces by surprise and they would not be taken by surprise a second time. All forces, regular and militia, were ordered to be ready to defend Niagara by all means necessary.

In the surrendering of the American forces on Queenston Heights, not all-American troops were captured. Some had made their way to the Niagara River, hoping to find a boat that would take them back to Lewiston. Others, not waiting for a boat, tried swimming across the fast-moving waters, only to drown in its icy grip. Still others made their way down the river towards what they thought were less patrolled areas, where they could wait until a more favorable time to cross.

A second order was issued by General Sheaffe that a search was to be made for escaped American soldiers. Those who refused to surrender were to be shot on site, no questions asked. All Americans were to be arrested and detained.

It was this order that reached the people of Queenston, that found its way to Mary Johnson and Nathan Douglas.

Attending his duties, the corporal of the 41st stationed at Queenston reorganized the troops and executed the standing orders from General Sheaffe. By the water's edge, the sentries were doubled and patrols around Queenston were increased. The fisherman's trail, used by the American soldiers to gain access above the redan, was made impassable. The only way to gain access now to the heights was through Queenston and through him.

A private, the one who had been patrolling with him the night before the invasion, came to him.

"Sir, do you remember a few days ago, we found this bloke sleeping down near the river?" he asked.

"You mean by that building that got blown away?" he said.

"Yes, sir. Where do you think he came from? He said that he was from St. Davids and was here to see Miss Johnson. What do you think?"

The corporal stood for a moment, thinking about what he said.

"Yea, I remember him. I also remember his accent. It had a drawl about it, like he was not from these parts."

"Where do you think he went?" the private asked. "When we were chasing those Americans, I saw him off in the woods. Looked like he was with Miss Johnson and Miss Secord. What say we go have a look?" And with that, they made their way to the Secord's home.

Laura Secord had done her best to repair the broken door, secure the windows and try to get the home ready for winter weather. It was hard without her husband to help, but James, needing constant care, still lay on the makeshift bed. But at least the fever had broken, and he was semi-awake. As the soldiers approached, they saw a wisp of smoke rising from the chimney.

"Looks like they ain't gone anywhere," the private said.

The corporal only grunted as they neared the door of the Secord home.

"Mama, it's soldiers," said Mary, the oldest of the five children. "They say they want to talk with you."

Laura Secord had been attending to her husband, trying to get some soup into him as she carefully placed the ladle near his lips, head gently tilted forward.

"I will be with you in a moment," she said. "Please, come in."

The corporal entered the Secord home as the private waited outside.

"How is he?" the corporal asked. He had seen too many battles and too many wounded soldiers. It was all too familiar.

"He's better, thank you," Laura said as she gently laid James' head back on the pillow. "The doctor says that it will be a long road to recovery. One day at a time."

Laura looked at him as she continued. "But I'm sure that you are not here to check on my husband. Is there anything that I can help you with?"

"General Sheaffe has ordered that we are to keep a lookout for any American soldiers who may have escaped. Have you seen anyone around, anyone who may seem out of place? Can't be too safe," he said.

"No, I have little time to go out and my children have said nothing. No one has troubled us if that's what you mean."

"What about that stranger, the one who was with Miss Johnson? He said he was from St. Davids. You remember him, don't you?" Looking over at James, he went on. "Didn't he come to the barracks and help you carry your husband? You know who I mean, don't you? I can ask the private, here. He carried the other end, if you wish."

"No need. Yes, he helped me bring James here and helped keep the children safe. I don't know where he came from, and I don't know where he went. All I know is that he was here when we needed help," she said, turning back to her husband.

"Begging your pardon, ma'am," he said. "We can't have no strangers wandering these parts. There's enough trouble brewing without strangers. Where can I find him?"

Laura had James' head tilted once more as she sought to get some nourishment into him.

"I don't know. Maybe he's still around. Maybe he's left these parts. I have enough to do without worrying about who may or may not be here."

The corporal knew that the conversation had ended. Laura was going to give him no further information. If this stranger was to be found, then he must find him.

The Hamilton estate was no more. That was obvious, as it lay in a pile of rubble. The corporal knew that Mary Johnson's father lived in St. Davids. He had seen him, even chatted with him when he would bring his produce into Queenston to sell.

Leaving the Secord home, he turned to the private.

"Get some men together. We are going to St. Davids to see if we can find this stranger that seems to have vanished," he ordered.

"Now, sir?" the private asked. "It's going to be dark in an hour."

"Have your men ready by six a.m. No later. We're going a hunting."

Chapter 32

Becky had pulled the wagon around the back of the small homestead in St. Davids. She knew the routine. It was always the same. George would go into the house and bring her back an apple. As she quickly devoured the treat, he would release her from her harness, dress her down, and release her into the makeshift stable. It wasn't much, but it kept the biting wind from bringing frostbite.

Becky had been with the Johnson household since Mary was a young girl. A neighbor had faced the same financial troubles that all the homesteaders seemed to face. Money was tight, crops were lean, and children needed to be fed. They sold what they could and kept what was necessary to survive.

George had brought this nameless foal home. Lifting Mary in his arms, she stroked its ears and rubbed its neck.

"What should we call her?" he asked little Mary.

"Do you think mama would be mad if we called her Becky?" she asked. "She's as beautiful as you tell me my mama was, though, a horse. Do you think that would be okay, papa?"

"I think your mother would be proud," he said, pulling her tight.

George watched as Becky slowly made her way around the stall, seeking to find a place where she might rest after the day's events. She no longer bounded like she did as a young horse, but then neither did he. They had grown old together and had shared the loneliness of Mary leaving home.

But here was his Mary, back again. Only she was not alone. Who was this stranger? George had never seen him before on his many travels to Queenston, never saw him at the estate, never heard of him before Mary brought him to his home. She said that he saved her life.

As George pondered over the mysterious visitor and his daughter's unexpected connection to him, a sense of curiosity gnawed at him, urging him to unravel the enigma that Nathan represented. Yet, practical matters demanded attention first.

"But for now, there were chores to be done," George mused to himself. "The cows need to be milked and fed, the eggs gathered, and the chickens cooped up for the night. Then we will talk," he resolved, determined to uncover the truth about Mary's companion.

Meanwhile, Mary bustled about the kitchen, preparing the evening meal, her mind occupied with the tasks at hand. As George entered, she turned to greet him, a warm smile lighting up her face, momentarily setting aside the questions that lingered in both their minds.

"Everyone bedded down for the night?" she asked.

"All is done. Been a long day," he said. "I think Becky was ready to be home. She ain't quite got the same energy she once had. I know just how she feels," he said, tiredly placing himself down on his favorite chair.

"Where's Nathan? He's still here, isn't he?"

"I think he said that he wanted to get some firewood for tonight. I thought I heard some chopping a while ago."

Just as she had finished talking, Nathan came through the door, carrying an armful of cut wood.

"Thought we might need this for tonight," he said. "I can feel something blowing in from the north."

Piling the wood at the side of the fireplace, he placed a log on it as he stirred the embers to life.

George watched Nathan, somewhat lost to the moment. His mind was filled with the solemn events in Newark; with learning that this debt that had almost crippled his future was gone; with not knowing how to begin a conversation that he wanted to have, that he felt he should have. He loved his Mary and would not want to drive her away from him and into the arms of this stranger. He must take it slow.

Mary had walked around behind George, putting her hands on his shoulders, and squeezing. Leaning down, she kissed him on the cheek. "I love you, papa and I always will."

George's body quaked a little, not so much from the squeeze of Mary's fingers, but from the chill of the day. He knew he had been underdressed for this time of year, but the sun had shone brightly_as they journeyed into Newark. Yet it was that wind that seemed to penetrate through, seemed to tear at the weak places in his clothing. The chill got into him. Maybe crawling into the warmth of his bed, piled high with blankets, will take it away. For now, it's time to eat and relax.

"So, Mary said that you are a sailor. You must love the water," George said, trying to find a way into a conversation that he wanted, without getting right to the point.

"Yes, sir. There is something about being on the open seas, nothing but water below and wind above. There is a freedom that nothing else can bring," Nathan said, with a far-off look.

"Never been much for the water," George said. "Like to have my feet on solid ground."

"Where did you sail from? Got any port, in particular? I think Mary said that you brought supplies to the Hamilton estate, is that right?" George queried.

Nathan felt himself tensing up a little, shifting slightly in his chair. Mary only sat and listened. What else could she do?

"I sailed out of Oswego," he said, "Aboard the Peggy. She is a merchant ship owned by Mr. McNair. I was the first mate."

"Oswego. Isn't that an American port, somewhere up by Sacket's Harbor?" George asked.

"Yes, sir. Just south of Sacket's."

"So, does that make you an American?" George continued. "I can't see any British sailing on an American vessel."

"Yes, sir, I am. My parents live in Burlington, Vermont."

"Vermont. Never been to Vermont. Been to Albany but never Vermont," George continued to press for little points of entry into Nathan's life. He saw this young man feeling restless.

Don't want to drive him away, George thought to himself, but I need to know more.

"Mary said that you saved her life when the Estate got blown up. Is that right? How come you were there and not with the American army?" George said.

"Just curious," he added, as he looked across at Mary.

"The ship, the Peggy, brought supplies to Queenston in May," Nathan said. "With President Madison declaring war, the Peggy was dry docked. My sailing days were done, at least for now." Nathan shot a furtive glance towards Mary. George was quick to notice.

"So it wasn't just supplies that brought you back to Queenston," George said with a twinkle.

"Yes, sir. Well, no, sir. I knew that the army, the American army was preparing for war. I knew Mary was all alone in that big house and she was in danger if she stayed there." Nathan, by this time, was getting quite jittery.

"So you thought you would rescue her?" George asked. "Were there no other people who could have done that?"

Mary started to said something when Nathan pushed away from the table.

"Sir, I am sorry if I have offended you. I only wanted to protect Mary from harm's way. I will leave if that is what you want." Grabbing his coat, Nathan moved towards the door.

Mary stood there speechless, feeling caught between these two worlds, not knowing what to say or what to do.

"Now hold on a minute," George said. "Sensitive, are we? Where are you going to go at this time of night? The nearest place is Queenston or Newark and I don't think there is much left in Queenston for you to go back to. You can stay here tonight. We can talk more in the morning."

George pushed back his chair, making his way to his bed. Within a short time, he was snoring, oblivious to any conversation Mary would have with Nathan.

Mary moved towards Nathan as she pulled him close.

"I am sorry," she said.

"Do you think he knows? Do you think he suspects?" Nathan asked. "Maybe it is better if I leave."

"Like he said, where are you going to go at this time of night? No, stay here. We will work it out in the morning."

Mary tossed some blankets, before settling into her own bed. This has been enough for one day. Tomorrow will take care of itself. At least, that's what she told herself.

Chapter 33

George had been up early as he made his way for his morning routines. The stable door had nudged partly open, allowing the stiff wind to push its way toward Becky. He made his way to where she stood, trying to stay away from the wind.

"Ah, Becky, I'm sorry. I thought I had latched it better," he said as he took a blanket and gently placed it over her back. "Here, this will keep you warm." George pulled Becky's head towards him as he nestled his own into hers.

"What would I ever do without you?" he added.

Adding straw to her manger, he made his way over towards his milking cows. Their udders were warm; their milk bountiful as the pails quickly filled, steaming as the cold air touched their warmth.

"Maybe I'll take some milk over to Mrs. Carter," he said out loud. "Her five kids could probably use some of this. Maybe later."

George was trying to keep his mind occupied, trying to somehow not think too much about the conversation that he wanted to have with Nathan, but it kept creeping in.

As he made his way towards the chicken coop, George looked out across the lane. There, walking, actually marching, were five soldiers heading his way. He thought he could recognize the one in front. He had a familiar look about him. Then he realized it was the corporal from Queenston. No soldiers make their way out this far unless they got soldiering on their mind.

In his house was Mary's friend, who was an American. It was the Americans who had just invaded Niagara and been defeated. They wouldn't take too kindly to this American in his house, let alone take too kindly to him keeping this American in his house.

Keeping tight to the outside of the house, George pushed his way through a slightly ajar door.

"Nathan, Nathan, get up. The soldiers are coming. You need to get up, now," George said as he nudged him with his hand.

Nathan jolted upright, moving towards the window to see these soldiers nearing the lane, heading to the Johnson homestead.

"Come, you can't go out the front. They will see you. I have a place that you can hide until they are gone, but you must trust me and move quickly," George whispered.

By this time, Mary had awakened and was standing near the table, a scared look upon her face. "Mary, get dressed and, for heaven's sake, get rid of that look. They will know something's up."

There was a small trapdoor beneath the edge of George's bed that led to a cold cellar below. "You can never be too cautious in these parts," he said. "Climb down. You will be safe," he said, tossing down some of his own blankets for warmth. Nathan squeezed his way through the trapdoor as George placed the bed securely back on top. Quickly making sure that nothing was out of the ordinary, he made his way to where Mary now stood. The soldiers arrived and, with a rap on the
door, both George and Mary took a deep breath.

"Good morning, corporal," he said. "What brings you a way out here? Little far from Queenston, isn't it?" he said, trying to be as normal as possible.

"Beg your pardon, sir. We are looking for someone, someone who was with your daughter, Mary, in Queenston a few days ago. Can I come in?"

George stepped back as the corporal and the private made their way into the house. One soldier remained outside the door while the other two made their way around the back, towards the stable.

"Miss," the corporal said to Mary. "We're looking for a stranger from Queenston who said that he had business with you. Is he with you now?"

"Stranger, stranger," she said, trying to be normal, but her voice was strained.

"You remember," the corporal went on.

"I also saw him with you and the Secord family. You know, in the woods just outside the town as the battle was fought. He also helped the private here carry Mr. Secord up to their home on a stretcher. Surely you haven't forgotten, have you?" he said with a sneer.

"You don't have to be rude about it," she said. "Yes, he was with me in Queenston and helped us save the lives of the Secord family. But he is not here now."

"Strange," the corporal continued. "I know I saw you in Newark, you know, at General Brock's funeral. I saw Mr. Johnson there and some other man. Who might that have been?"

"There were many people in Newark for the funeral," George said as he stepped in to protect his daughter.

"Yeah, but not all of them were with you. You don't mind if we have a look around, do you?" It wasn't a question as much as move and let us search.

In George's haste to hide Nathan, he had forgotten to remove the blankets that Nathan had used for a bed near the fireplace.

"What's this?" the corporal asked. "Why are these here?"

"I'm not feeling well," George stated. "I caught something yesterday and couldn't shake it, so I slept by the fireplace. I can't seem to get warm."

Where he slept was a lie. His not feeling well was the truth. George had become fevered. Mary moved towards him, placing her hand on his forehead as she felt his clammy skin.

"Papa, you're warm."

Turning to the corporal, she stared him in the eyes, challenging him to call her a liar.

"Do what you must and be quick about it. My papa is not feeling well and must rest."

"We will be done when we are done," the corporal replied, almost ignoring her.

"Corporal, remember that General Brock was a friend of mine, that Captain Hamilton and the Hamilton estate have been my benefactor. I am sure that General Sheaffe would be attentive to any concerns or improprieties that you might show

towards me or my papa," she said, almost with a threatening tone.

The corporal stared at her for a moment, before turning towards the private.

"Check those rooms there and be quick about it. We haven't got all day."

The private pulled back the sheets dividing the rooms, looking under the beds as George breathed softly and waited.

"Nothing here, sir," he said.

The corporal stood for a moment, looking around the home, seeking for any place that a man might hide. Seeing nothing, he ordered the private outside.

Without a word, he stepped outside and closed the door behind him. The five soldiers met in the lane to begin their trek back towards Queenston. For the moment Nathan was safe, but it was now becoming more dangerous for an American to remain in Niagara. He must either leave or find another way to remain hidden from military eyes.

George watched as the soldiers were nearly out of sight before he moved towards where Nathan was hiding. Pushing aside the bed, he pulled open the trapdoor. Nathan squeezed out of the darkness below, George's blankets in tow behind him.

"You heard?" George asked.

"Yes," he whispered. "I cannot put your lives in jeopardy or ask you to lie for me. I will wait until tonight and make my way elsewhere. Please don't ask where I might go. It would be better not to know so that you do not have to lie."

George and Mary said nothing. They knew he was right. What more could they add? Mary had so wanted to settle down here with Nathan, at least for a while, until she could decide what to do. But now it was not possible. At least they have today, while it is still light.

Chapter 34

The corporal and four privates had planned to make their way back towards Queenston from St. Davids. Honestly, he did not believe George or Mary Johnson about not knowing where this stranger was that had been seen with them. He may not have been found at the Johnson home, but that doesn't mean that he wasn't there. They just didn't find where he was hidden.

The corporal was a seasoned soldier and not easily threatened. Mary may have thought she could unsettle him by threatening him with General Sheaffe, but the General was a man of action, not sentiment. If the corporal could capture this stranger and bring him to the General, there just may be some reward for his due diligence.

The Johnson homestead was situated east of St. Davids, past where Four Mile Creek Road and York Road intersected. As the five soldiers headed away from the Johnson home, the corporal decided upon a plan of action that even he thought was ingenious. He knew the Johnsons would assume that these soldiers would return by the way they came, along the road that led towards Queenston. If the stranger tried to escape, he surely wouldn't go back through Queenston. They knew his face. He probably wouldn't risk going the way of Newark. The military were on the watch for those who were unknown, to strangers in their midst. No, the best way to go unnoticed was by either traveling down Four Mile Creek Road or towards Homer. Homer would lead deeper into Upper Canada territory. The most reasonable way of escape for this stranger would be Four Mile Creek Road.

Nathan watched the soldiers leave from the safety of the Johnsons' home, but also realized the imminent danger lurking outside. The corporal and his men had changed course, likely plotting to capture him, and Nathan knew he couldn't risk being seen while daylight still lingered.

Nathan quickly weighed his options. Remaining indoors until darkness fell seemed the wisest course of action, despite the potential for raising suspicions from Mary's father, George Johnson. Yet, the alternative of venturing outside and facing the lurking threat of the British soldiers held even greater peril.

As he grappled with this dilemma, Nathan found little solace in the thought of either confronting the British army or navigating the mounting concerns of Mary's father. Each path seemed fraught with uncertainty and danger, leaving him feeling trapped between the two formidable adversaries.

George's fever had quickly brought on the chills and aches of something more than just a common cold. He had developed a cough that would break out into coughing spells. The only place he felt warm was by the fire, bundled beneath the blankets. But though his body felt weakened, his mind was still sharp, seeking answers from this stranger in his house.

"Nathan," George said, "Come and sit with me by the fire. There is little else to do. The chores are done. Let's chat."

Mary tensed up a bit. She had grown up with her papa's "Let's chat" moments. He had a way of getting her to talk, of somehow finding his way into her soul and

bringing out those things she would rather have hidden. Like the time she got mad at Becky and threw some eggs at her, breaking them against her body. Her papa, over the evening meal, asked her how her day had been, whether she could get any eggs from the coop and how her time was grooming Becky. She just knew that he knew. It was better to fess up than face his questions. Now it was Nathan's turn, and she was squirming for him.

Nathan pulled up a chair near the fire, not too close to George. The chair was at an angle, away from where George was sitting. It's not that Nathan didn't want to be too close to George if he started coughing. It was that he didn't want to look him square in the eyes, to have those deep brown eyes penetrating through his defenses.

"So Nathan," George began. "Why did you choose to be a sailor? I'm sure that a fine, young man like yourself could have done many things with your life."

"As I said before, my folks are from Burlington, Vermont, near Lake Champlain. As a young boy, I felt drawn to the waters, watching the ships as the merchants gathered to receive their cargo. There is something romantic about the waters, almost seductive."

Nathan quickly caught himself. He needed to choose his words more carefully. The last thing he wanted was a misunderstanding of intentions with George's daughter, Mary.

"I can appreciate that," George said. "When I get onto the land and the soil's turned, the crops planted, well, it's like a love language that calls to me. So tell me, what do your parents do in Burlington?"

"They own and manage a store. They trade with not only the local folk, but even as far away as Montreal, at least before the war broke out. I haven't been home since it started, so I'm hoping that everything is still okay."

"Yes, it's hard for parents when their children are far away, but they grow up too quickly and must make a life for themselves," George said, turning towards Mary.

She smiled at her papa, but George knew she was anxious. She knew something that he didn't know yet about this Nathan fellow. Time to press a little more.

"Was your family always from Burlington?" he asked.

Nathan suddenly felt this lump in his throat. He took on a nervous cough as Mary went to get him water.

"Hope you're not getting what I've got," George said, as Nathan took a deep drink from the cup. He could only offer a forced smile.

"Mr. Johnson, I respect you. I really do, and I care for your daughter. Mary is a fine woman, a credit to her upbringing and your care. As I told her at the estate, I do not want any secrets between us. I think I know what you want to know. You want to know my story and it isn't pretty. In fact, I am ashamed of things that happened, but I can't change anything."

George suddenly went quiet as he stared into the dancing embers.

"Yes, my parents live in Burlington, but they did not always live there. They moved there from Albany after their parents died, following the War of Independence. I know you see it as a revolution. They saw it as a liberation from British dominance. Their parents were merchants in Albany. That's where my dad learned how to manage a store."

Mary, by now, had gotten up and made her way into the kitchen area. There was little to do since she had cleaned up earlier. She just didn't want to be near if things got heated by the fireplace.

"You probably have heard that my last name is Douglas and yes, your family knew my grandparents. They were the ones that your parents did business with and at one time were friends with. The war changed all that, as it has changed things here as well."

"I will leave if you want me to go," Nathan offered, but George said nothing as he continued to stare into the fire.

"I know about the Safety Committee. I know about the people, such as your family, as well as many others, whose loyalties were questioned and who were forced from their lands. I know it was hard."

George turned slightly towards Nathan, stopping him from continued.

"You know nothing," George said. "You weren't even born when my parents were forced from their home. We had a knock on our door at night, warning us that your grandfather was coming with armed guards to arrest my father and take our land. We had to flee with nothing but the clothes we wore. Everything they had worked to build was gone: their home, their land, their crops, their livestock. Everything was gone, so please, do not tell me how hard it was. I was there."

"Nathan," George said, "I am a man of my word, and you are welcome to stay here until dark."

George pushed the blankets off his shoulders and rose. Grabbing his cloak, he made his way towards the door and to the stall. Piling the surrounding hay, he pulled his cloak tight, waiting for nightfall to come.

Neither Mary nor Nathan knew what to say. She had warned him that the pain still ran deep. George had known much loss, in Albany and here in St. Davids. Nathan's presence only reminded him of how deep that loss was.

"I am sorry," Mary finally said.

"I am as well," Nathan said. "Mary, I can't stay here. Would you come with me? The Hamilton estate is gone. We could travel to Burlington. I could work for my dad. We could build a life for ourselves. You would love Vermont." Nathan had taken both of Mary's hands in his as he tried to look her in the eyes, but she would not hold his gaze.

"Nathan," she said, "My life is here. My papa is here, and he needs me. I can't just walk out and leave all this behind."

"What if I need you?" Nathan whispered. "What if I want to spend my life with you? Does that not mean anything to you?"

She could say little as he dropped her hands, reached for his coat and slipped out the door. The afternoon shadows were lengthening as the sun dipped behind the hills of St. Davids. Nathan had to decide quickly which way to go. Queenston was not an option. Newark posed too big a risk. Homer would take him further away. Four Mile Creek Road, that is where he will go. Follow it down to Chippewa and then Erie, make his way across to Black Rock and then home. With that he set out, not knowing if the path home would yet be filled with danger.

Chapter 35

George sat quietly in Becky's stall, hay and cloak pulled tightly around him. His mind swirled as he replayed the conversation with Nathan over and over again. He knew Nathan was not much older than his own daughter and that the events that destroyed his family in Albany were not Nathan's events. How could they be? He wasn't even born. But these were the events of the Douglas family and Nathan was a Douglas. Same story, same family. How could he be guiltless and yet?

George plucked a piece of hay and twirled it with his teeth. His eyes were closed as his mind played out his story, the story of his family. He never heard Becky slowly walking towards him. But he felt this cold nuzzle on his face and the piece of hay plucked from his lips. The full side of Becky's face pressed against his, playfully giving him a nudge. Reaching up and wrapping his arm around her neck, he pulled her tight as he wept softly.

Using the horse's neck, George pulled himself up, stroking Becky's mane.

"How could I hang on to this for so long?" he finally said, with only Becky to listen. "What is done is done. Sure, it hurts, but I can't go back and undo it. I so miss my papa and mama. I miss my Rebecca, but I still have Mary. Please, let her be there when I go back in."

George pushed open the stall door and tightly fastened it behind him, making his way towards the door of the home. He was unsure if anyone would still be there, if his Mary would be there. He just hoped that he wasn't too late.

Mary clung to her father, seeking solace in his comforting embrace. She couldn't shake the overwhelming sense of turmoil that engulfed her. Nathan's absence weighed heavily on her heart, leaving her feeling adrift and uncertain. Yet, in the warmth of her father's arms, she found a fleeting sense of reassurance amidst the chaos.

"Papa, papa." Her voice choked with emotion. George held her close, his embrace a silent promise of steadfast support and unwavering love. In that tender moment, Mary felt a glimmer of hope flicker within her, a beacon of light in the darkness of uncertainty.

Meanwhile, the corporal and his men, having left the Johnson home empty-handed, remained undeterred in their pursuit of Nathan. Despite their initial setback, the corporal was resolute in his determination to capture the elusive stranger. With a steely resolve, he knew that the hunt for Nathan was far from over—it had only just begun.

Having made their way to where Four Mile Creek Road came into St. Davids, they continued to follow it. They snaked their way along the base of the escarpment to where it began its ascent upward. The corporal's goal was to find two vantage points where he might place his men. It was no good having the five of them together. If this stranger was fleet of foot, he might easily escape their trap. It would be better to position them so that they are both behind and in front, thus creating a pincer move, capturing his prey.

"You two," he ordered, "remain here, but stay hidden. I know the night is going to get cold. No fires, do you understand? Let the stranger pass, but follow at a distance. Do not allow him to see you."

They nodded as the other three moved farther up the hill. About halfway, he positioned two more soldiers, giving the same order. He himself was going to continue another hundred yards, just in case.

As the shadows lengthened, the sun slowly descended in the western sky. The moon's rays danced behind soft, floating clouds, creating a silhouette of patterns.

With a heavy heart, Nathan departed from the Johnson homestead, the weight of disappointment and rejection bearing down on him. The encounter with Mary's father had unfolded just as he had feared, the outcome aligning all too closely with the narrative he had envisioned. As he walked away, a somber acceptance settled over him, acknowledging the reality of his situation.

Resigned to the fact that Mary's father had judged him based on his family's troubled history, Nathan couldn't help but feel a sense of sorrow and regret. The script he had expected had played out before him, leaving him grappling with the painful realization that he was no longer welcomed in the home he had hoped to find solace in.

Meanwhile, unbeknownst to Nathan, a trap had been laid by the soldiers, concealed in various hiding spots, eagerly expecting his arrival. As Nathan wrestled with his emotions, unaware of the danger lurking nearby, the stage was set for a confrontation that would alter the course of events yet again.

He had hoped that Mary might feel differently. They were now both adults, having made their own way in life. Neither lived in their parents' home. Neither were accountable to their parents. Both needed to make a life of their own, find a soul mate and raise a family. Since Nathan first saw her the previous May, he thought maybe she would be the one to share life with him. He had risked his own life to save her at the Hamilton estate. With the Secord children, he had provided her help. He had done everything that he could to show her he cared about her. Surely the kiss at the estate, the holding of hands and showing affection was enough to win her heart.

But family ties run deep. Nathan never considered that when he asked her to leave with him, he was asking her to leave the father who had raised her, the homestead that she had helped to save, the life that she had known. She needed certainty in her life. He loved excitement. She longed for order. He could live with organized chaos. The world he had created in his mind differed from the real world that both lived in.

He never fully realized that he was asking her to choose between family and him. She chose family. He left, never knowing if he would ever return.

Traveling the road from St. Davids, he made his way along Four Mile Creek Road. He knew that this road was the best choice to make his way back to his homeland.

As a sailor, he was trained to be alert for any unexpected dangers. You never know when the winds may change, or unexpected events may come. But this day, his training was clouded by his thoughts of the recent events. He had never expected the unexpected. He was not paying attention to his surroundings. The dancing moonlight would not hide him as he made his way to the base of the hill.

The first posted sentries, hidden by the trees, watched as Nathan neared. The orders, by the corporal, were to allow him to pass and then follow at a distance, staying
hidden along the edges of the tree line.

Nathan passed the first sentry post. The first two soldiers waited and then followed. Halfway up the hill, there was a shuffling sound, somewhere off to his left. With a start, he saw two soldiers quickly moving towards him. Behind him, the other sentries had left the tree line and were now racing up the hill. There was nowhere to go but up. Breaking out in a run, he paused as the corporal stepped in front, with bayonet fixed on his rifle.

"Halt, or I will stab you where you stand," the corporal ordered. "Then I may just shoot you for good measure."

Nathan was trapped as the soldiers came in behind, gasped for breath. The burlier of the four knocked him to the ground, searching his pockets and waist for any hidden weapon. He had nothing. He had needed nothing but his wits to defend himself.

For a moment, the corporal thought about continuing the journey, with a prisoner in tow, up Four Mile Creek Road, towards Portage Road and coming into Queenston from the heights above the village. But he had a change of mind, ordering them to go back the way they came.

"We need to show these homesteaders that they cannot hide these enemies from us. We will seek them out and we will find them," the corporal said, rather triumphantly.

The trap had been set and sprung. They now had their quarry. The corporal felt like it had been a good day soldiering as they made their turn at St. Davids and began the journey towards Queenston. The moon continued to dance behind the soft clouds on that crisp October night. The corporal thought it was a dance of joy.

Chapter 36

George Johnston had Becky hitched to the wagon as Mary made her way out the door. She had brought some extra blankets, laying them across the legs of her papa and herself. A heavier quilt was placed over the shoulders of George. He should be in bed, because his fever and cough had grown worse as the night wore on.

"Papa," Mary asked, "Should we not wait till morning when we can see better? Shouldn't you be in bed staying warm instead of out on this chilly night?"

"Mary," he said. "We need to find Nathan before anyone else finds him. I could not forgive myself if anything happened to him."

There was no sense arguing the point. They both wanted the same thing. With a flick of the reins, Becky began her pull on the wagon. At the edge of the lane, George gave a gentle pull to the right as they made their way towards St. Davids. George was thankful that the night was calm and the moon bright, though the night air was crisp. If Nathan is walking along the road, they should be able to find him before anyone else does.

As Becky continued her gentle trot down the road leading to Queenston, the Johnsons pressed onward, blissfully unaware of the soldiers trailing behind them, their prisoner in tow. The night enveloped them like a heavy cloak, its silence broken only by the rhythmic sound of Becky's hooves against the earth. Mary nestled closer to her father, seeking refuge from the chill that crept in with the darkness. Together, they ventured towards Queenston, each step bringing them closer to their destination, unaware of the converging paths that would soon unite them with others on the same journey.

George sat, almost stoic, as the wagon continued its journey. He was feeling a heaviness in his chest, a tightening. As he broke into coughing spells, he would turn his head away from Mary, but the sharpness of the pain took his breath away. But he would not turn back now. His eyes were sore, more tired than sore, from the strain of looking into the darkness, of the hour of the night, of the fever that had gripped his body.

As they neared Queenston, they were stopped by two soldiers on patrol.

"Halt, who goes there?" one asked, the other with rifle pointed.

"It is the Johnsons," Mary said. "George and Mary Johnson."

"What are you doing here at this time of night?" the private said. "No one should be out on the roads. Did you not hear that General Sheaffe has ordered a curfew?"

"No," Mary said. "My papa is sick, and I need to find the doctor. Please let us pass."

This wasn't the only reason they were on the road, but this much was true. George needed to see a doctor as he broke into another coughing spell.

The private moved closer to the wagon. He pushed aside the blankets, satisfying himself that no one else was with them.

"Go ahead," the private said as they lowered their weapons.

As George and Mary slowly approached the village of Queenston, their hearts heavy with concern for Nathan's whereabouts, they scanned the quiet streets, hoping to get a quick look at him. Yet Nathan remained elusive, his absence casting a shadow over their arrival. With George in need of urgent medical attention, they made their way to Doc Smith's house. Mary's eyes stayed fixed on the window as she prayed for Nathan's safe return.

The five soldiers trudged wearily towards Queenston, Nathan among them, the weight of the day bearing down heavily upon them all. Despite the corporal's efforts to maintain an air of discipline, exhaustion gnawed at their resolve, each step a struggle against fatigue. The village loomed ahead, offering the promise of rest, yet uncertainty lingered in the air, casting a pall over their weary procession.

The corporal allowed them to take a five-minute rest break every mile or so. But only five minutes. He knew that if they stayed any longer in any one place, sleep may overtake them, and the stranger would make his escape. They had worked too hard to capture their enemy. They can sleep later, after they have delivered him to the jail.

Finally, they could see the outline of houses in the village of Queenston. As they drew nearer, they were stopped by the same sentries on patrol.

"Halt, who goes there?" the private asked.

"Corporal Jones. We have a prisoner with us. Let us through," he ordered.

"Yes sir, but our orders are to escort any prisoners to the jail down by the barracks," the sentry said.

"We will deliver him ourselves. Stand down," the corporal order. "We didn't travel this far to let him into the hands of such as you."

The corporal's motives were more than just delivering a prisoner. He hoped that this action would find its way to General Sheaffe. There just may be a promotion for him.

"Are we the only ones to have come through here this night?" the corporal asked as they moved away.

"No sir. Mary and George Johnson came through by wagon a while ago.

They said that George needed to see a Doc Smith.”

“I bet they did,” the corporal added. “Did you actually see them go to Doc Smith’s?”

“No sir,” the private said.

The corporal’s gaze fixed on the houses in Queenston, looking for any sign that there may be others lingering. He knew Mary had friends in this village who would do anything for her. He wasn’t about to be ambushed, and his prisoner escaped by their meddling in his affairs.

“I am ordering you two to accompany us to the jail. Once the prisoner is secure, return to your posts,” the corporal commanded sternly.

“Yes, sir,” the private responded promptly, grateful for the break in the monotony of their patrol. With their orders clear, the group of eight soldiers proceeded towards the heart of Queenston, their mission to deliver Nathan to the jail. For Nathan, there was no hope of escape now, surrounded by seven soldiers determined to ensure his confinement.

Nathan trudged along reluctantly with the soldiers, his freedom stripped away by bayonets at his back. With every step, he felt the weight of his predicament bearing down upon him, knowing that any hesitation would be met with force.

His mind was tired from the constant stress of the past number of days. In some ways, he was glad the chase was over. He would rather have made his way home on his own terms, but at least he is still alive, even if he is in the hands of the British.

Hearing that the Johnsons were in Queenston to see Doc Smith brought concern to him. He had heard George coughing and knew that he was sick. Maybe he shouldn’t have left. He knew George was upset, but maybe they could have worked it out. Maybe George could have found it in his heart to forgive. But all his maybes amounted to nothing now. There was nothing more that he could do to help the Johnsons. He couldn’t even help himself.

The jail door swung open with a heavy clang, and Nathan was unceremoniously shoved inside, left to face the cold and uncertainty of his confinement. Alone in the stark cell, he huddled in a corner, his only solace the coat wrapped tightly around him. The chase had ended, and now he awaited an uncertain future, trapped in the confines of his prison.

Meanwhile, in Doc Smith’s examining room, George was being tended to while Mary anxiously waited in the foyer. Concern gnawed at her as she watched her father’s condition worsen. Standing near the window, she strained her eyes to catch any sign of improvement, but her gaze fell upon a disheartening sight. Soldiers, the same ones who had visited their home earlier, marched with purpose towards the river. Nathan was among them, his posture resigned to his fate. Mary's heart sank as she realized Nathan had been captured, his escape thwarted by the relentless pursuit of the soldiers.

She wanted to rush to them, to tell them they had made a mistake. Nathan wasn't like the American soldiers who had invaded. He had saved her life. He had risked all to help the Secords. He was a good man, but all she could do was stand there and watch.

Quickly, they passed out of her sight. Closing the door, she slumped in a chair. Putting her hands to her face, Mary sobbed. The lives of the two men that she cared about were now in danger, and there was very little she could do about it. She had never felt so helpless in all her life, so alone.

Chapter 37

Doc Smith made his way out of the examining room to where Mary sat. Handing her a towel, he waited until she had wiped her eyes and regained her composure.

"Mary," he said, "Your father is very sick. The cough has settled into his chest, and I am afraid it may get worse for him."

She still sat with her head cradled in her hands, listening to the seriousness of the Doc's words.

"He is close to having pneumonia. You need to get him home to bed and keep him warm. He must stay in bed. Is there anyone who can help you?" he asked.

Mary wanted to tell him that the only man who could help, the only other man that she really cared about, was now sitting in the jail for nothing more than being an American sailor.

"No," she finally said. "We have no one to help. I will take him home and do as you say."

Moving to the examining room, Mary helped her papa to his feet, wrapping the blankets tightly around him. Climbing up on the wagon, Mary now sat where her papa had sat before. With a flick of the reins, they began the long trek back home as her papa broke out into another coughing spell.

The morning light broke the darkness in the eastern skies as they turned onto the road that led to St. Davids and towards home. She was thankful that Becky needed little help to find her way. Mary closed her eyes as she drifted in and out of sleep. Home was just around the corner for them. Soon her papa would be nestled under his warm blankets. Soon, she would be busier than before, tending to the chores and caring for her papa alone. Her heart suddenly longed for Nathan, for what might have been and never knowing if she would ever see him again. She could only weep.

Becky pulled up to the door as Mary helped her papa off the wagon and into the house. By now, he had grown lethargic and moved with difficulty. Helping him into his bedroom, she gently laid him on his bed, covering him with his blankets. Before tending to Becky, she stoked the fire as she added more logs. Soon it sprang to life with warmth and light.

Becky had already made her way to the back of the house. It seemed like she, too, was glad to be home. Once unhitched, Becky made her way to the stall, Mary following. Taking the blanket, Mary gently placed it over her back.

The morning chores still awaited her. She had done this many times as a younger woman and knew the routine. Becky needed her hay for the day, the stall cleaned and fresh straw for her bed. The two cows needed to be milked, and the eggs gathered. She was thankful that it was now October. The last thing she wanted to do was tend to crops. Walking to the side of the house, Mary gathered more wood for the fire, placing these in the wood crib.

As Mary finally succumbed to exhaustion and lay down in her bed, intending to rest for just a moment, the weight of the day and the events of the long night pressed heavily upon her. Yet, what started as a short break turned into several hours of profound relaxation.

In Queenston, in the dim light of morning, Nathan stirred within his cramped cell, the dawn illuminating the bars of his prison but failing to dispel the darkness that weighed heavily on his heart. Despite the dawn's light filtering through the window facing the river, Nathan found little solace in the sight of Lewiston beyond. The remnants of a defeated plan lingered in the presence of the military and bateaux by the river's edge, but there was no sign of the organized troop movements that once threatened his freedom.

The jailer entered through the doorway. In the cell, next to him, were two other prisoners, wearing military uniforms, only not the uniforms of the American army. They were British regulars.

"The captain has ordered you two released," he said. "You are to report to him at once. So much for a drunken night out on the town."

They said little as they moved past the jailer. He was not their concern. They had yet to face the captain and British military justice was not for the faint of heart.

Turning to Nathan, the jailer, with a sneering voice, said, "Your turn is coming. The captain has ordered that you be taken to Fort George." With that, he was gone.

Nathan stood, looking longingly towards Lewiston, when the corporal and two privates appeared.

"This is your lucky day," the corporal said. "We get to take you to Fort George."

The jailer unlocked Nathan's cell as the private motioned for him to come out. Just for good measure, the private reminded Nathan what the point of a bayonet felt like with a small poke. Nathan winced with pain.

Outside the jail, an ammunition wagon awaited, a stark reminder of Nathan's newfound confinement. The corporal's laughter echoed as he secured Nathan's hands and feet, ensuring any thoughts of escape were futile. With a mixture of resignation and uncertainty, Nathan, once a respected first mate, now faced an uncertain future as they set off towards Fort George.

Meanwhile, Mary stirred from her slumber to the sound of a knock at the door, signaling the transition from early morning to the afternoon. Exhausted from the events of the previous night, she had slept deeply, finding temporary solace from the trials and tribulations that had beset her.

"Just a moment," she shouted.

She first needed to check on her papa to see if he was okay. Entering his room, she found him still asleep, but his pillow and bedding were soaked. He was sweating profusely. Feeling his forehead, he felt like he was burning up.

"Come in," she said as she moved towards the kitchen.

Filling a small pail with water and grabbing a cloth, she made her way back towards his bedroom as the visitor entered. It was Mrs. Carter.

"Mary, I heard George was not well. Can I see if there is anything that I can do to help?" she asked.

"Mrs. Carter, please come in. Papa is fevered and I need to get his fever down. I hope this cold compress will help. His bed is wet from his sweat and needs to be changed."

"Here, let me help." Mrs. Carter took the pail and compress, making her way to George. "We need to get these bedsheets off and dry things for him. Do you have any more that we can use?"

Mary stood for a moment, not sure what to do. She had felt overwhelmed by Nathan leaving and seeing him captured, by her father's sickness, by the chores. She was grateful for Mrs. Carter, almost taking over for her, but this is her papa. Shouldn't she be attending to his needs, trying to get him well?

Mrs. Carter seemed to almost know what she was thinking.

"Mary, when my husband, John, was sick, I didn't know what to do. We had five children to raise, and I just knew that I couldn't lose John. Who would take care of us? Who would help me raise our children? But as John got sicker and weaker, your papa just one day showed up, unannounced. He took Andrew and Betsy, my two oldest, to help with the chores. When John could no longer till our soil and plant the crops, George was there to help. Then John died. It was the worst day of my life. George said nothing, but got the preacher from Newark and helped me bury my husband. I didn't think I could go on. It was your papa who helped me and gave me hope."

Mrs. Carter, by now, had stripped the bed of its linens and replaced them with clean linens. She then removed George's clothes, replacing them with dry clothes.

"Forgive me, Mary," she said. "But you're his daughter and shouldn't have to look on. He is going to need some broth. Can you get that ready so that I can feed him? Unless, of course, you want to do this."

Mary smiled as she made her way to the kitchen to do as she was asked. She thought about how little she knew about her papa. She knew how much he loved to help others, of how generous he was and caring for those in need. But she also knew how lonely he was and wondered why he had never remarried after her mother died.

"Thank you for coming," Mary said. "What about your children? Will they be okay until you get back?"

"Yes, they will be fine. Andrew and Betsy, God bless them, have been such a help. They will look after things until I return. Right now, your papa needs me. Will you allow me to help?" Mrs. Carter asked as she brought the linens and laid them by the fireplace.

"Yes, yes. I am most grateful for your help," Mary replied as she brought a cup of broth.

"Here, let me feed him." Mrs. Carter took the cup from Mary. "Would you be able to wash out those linens, so we have clean ones for when he needs to be changed again?"

Mary said little. She gathered up the bedding to soak in a bucket of water. She will hang these to dry once Mrs. Carter leaves.

"Oh, by the way," Mary said, "I have some milk for you to take home. I know that papa would have done this if he was better."

Mary smiled as she busied herself with cleaning linens. Her thoughts drifted to the prospect of Mrs. Carter becoming her father's wife. Perhaps, she mused, Nathan's unexpected presence had paved the way for her father to leave the past behind and embrace a brighter future. It was a hopeful notion, one that she clung to dearly as she went about her chores.

Meanwhile, the ammunition wagon carrying Nathan neared Fort George as the afternoon sun cast its warm glow upon the landscape. Despite the discomfort of being bound and jostled along the journey, Nathan's thoughts lingered on the events that had led him to this moment. As the wagon came to a halt near the north-east corner of the fort, memories of past visits flooded his mind, reminders of the fallen heroes whose final resting place lay within the bastion's walls.

"Time to get out and face real military justice," the corporal said. "You can join your friends who thought that they could invade our land."

Unhooking Nathan from the ring lock, with hands still tied together, the corporal half-dragged him from the back of the wagon, causing him to tumble to the ground.

"Get up," he said.

Major Glegg had watched the wagon enter and Nathan being

unceremoniously dropped by his feet.

"Get up," the corporal shouted again.

Nathan stumbled to his feet, his legs a bit wobbly beneath him.

"What do we have?" Major Glegg asked the corporal.

"We caught this stranger fleeing from St. Davids. He has been lurking around before the invasion. I think he is a spy for the Americans," the corporal offered.

"Are you a spy?" Major Glegg asked.

"No sir, I am not," Nathan answers. "I came to warn Mary Johnson that the Americans were going to invade and that she was not safe. My only concern was warning her. I had no part in the invasion."

"Would she vouch for you?" Major Glegg asked. "We will see. Place him with the other prisoners until we can decide. But if you are a spy, you will be hung."

Major Glegg watched as the corporal escorted Nathan towards the prisoner compound. The fate of Nathan Douglas now lay in the hands of others, his future uncertain and beyond Major Glegg's control.

Meanwhile, Mrs. Carter remained at George's bedside, tending to him with care and dedication. Over the course of a few hours, she changed cold compresses, offered nourishing broth, and ensured his comfort as best she could. Though George remained feverish, there were signs of improvement, his cough subsiding and his condition gradually easing.

"I think that I have done all that I can do for today," she said. "I need to go home and see to my children. George seems to have gotten through the worse of it. You should be okay for tonight. I will come back tomorrow after the chores are done."

As she made her way to the door, Mary asked her to wait.

"Here is that milk I promised you. We have some extra bread and sausage. I know papa would want you to have it. You have been a big help to us. Thank you."

Mrs. Carter graciously accepted the provisions offered to her, bidding farewell as she departed to attend to her own family. Mary tended to the fire, adding another log before preparing herself for the evening chores that awaited her. With Becky needing to be settled for the night, the cows to be milked, and the eggs gathered, Mary set about her tasks with a sense of purpose, hopeful that the worst was now behind them and that her father's condition would continue to improve with each passing day.

The next morning dawned crisp and clear. Mary had already completed her chores by the time a private from Fort George arrived at her home.

"Sorry to trouble you at this time of the morning, miss," the private said.

Mary said nothing. She had nothing to say to the military. Her experience with the corporal at this very place left her somewhat resentful of their intrusions into their lives.

"Major Glegg is requesting that you come to Fort George. There is a prisoner who says he knows you. The major wants to make sure before he passes sentence upon him."

A wave of anxiety quickly passed over her. Sentencing for what?

"Who is it this person and what kind of sentence?" she asked.

"It's not for me to say, miss. The major is requesting your presence on this day. What shall I tell the major?"

She couldn't just leave. Her papa was still quite sick and needing her constant care, but she knew that the only prisoner who would know her was Nathan. Mrs. Carter had said that she would be back to help care for her papa. If she would help, then maybe she can get away.

"Private," Mary said. "My papa is very sick. I need you to stay here with him while I go to see if a neighbor will help me. Can you do that for me?"

"Yes, miss. I will wait but don't be long. I need to give your answer to Major Glegg by mid-afternoon."

Mary grabbed her coat and quickly exited the door, making her way to Mrs. Carter's small homestead. By the time she arrived, she was breathless. She knocked and waited. Andrew opened the door to her.

"I am Mary, Mary Johnson. I need to see your mother right away. Is she here?" Mary said, looking past him.

"Mama, there's a Mary Johnson to see you," Andrew shouted.

"Let her in. I'll be with you in a moment."

The Carter home was smaller than the one she grew up in. There were three small cots lined together in one space and two in another. A larger bed was off to the right, curtain drawn.

The curtain was pushed aside as Mrs. Carter, with a small child in her arms, made her way towards Mary.

"Sorry," she said. "I needed to change young William. Is your papa okay? Has anything happened?"

"No, he is still sick, but better. Thank you for your help yesterday."

"I was glad to help, but is that why you are here? Is there something that I can do for you?" Mrs. Carter gave William to Andrew as she took Mary's hand.

"Mrs. Carter. I don't know how to ask this, so I'll just do it. There is a friend of mine who is being held prisoner at Fort George. A private is at my house now to see if I will come and vouch for him before they sentence him.”

“You need me to sit with your father?”

“Could you? I know it is asking much. I will try to be as quick as I can.”

“Yes, I will come,” she said. “I may need to take my two youngest with me. They will be quiet. Andrew and Betsy can look after things here. Let me get some things ready and I will be over shortly.”

The private was still waiting for Mary by the laneway.

“I have found someone to look after my papa so I can go,” she said.

“Okay, miss. I will tell the Major that you will be there.”

“Wait. You might as well travel with me. I will hitch up the horse and wagon as soon as Mrs. Carter comes, unless you can stay a little longer with papa while I do this.”

Mary attached the harness, gently walking horse and wagon to the front. By this time, Mrs. Carter had arrived with her two youngest. Placing them near the fire, she went to attend to George. Mrs. Carter picked up as if she had never left, as if this was where she really belonged. Mary knew her papa was in good hands. Leaving with the private, she began the journey to Fort George.

Chapter 38

Nathan had been taken to a compound with the other prisoners. He hadn't eaten since the previous morning, so when the prisoners were ordered to line up to receive their supper portions, he was well ready. It wasn't much, a smaller portion than he was used to: a piece of bread, some lentil soup and a small piece of jerky, but at least it was something.

There was little to do. Some soldiers gathered in small groups and talked about home. Others sat by themselves. Some here, some there, but all stuck in that small, confined area.

Nathan knew no one in that group. No one knew him. The prisoners had become suspicious of any newcomers, such as Nathan, being in their midst. The British were not unknown to place spies among the prisoners to glean information from the troops, such as escape plans. Taking a corner by himself, he sat on the cold ground, thinking of what was and what may yet be his fate. He tried to push aside the thought of a hangman's noose, that this may be his end. How he missed Vermont.

A fellow prisoner, an officer, sat down beside him. Pulling up his pant leg up, he reached into his sock and took out some paper. The pages had writing on them, though Nathan couldn't make out what was written. The officer twirled the paper with his fingers as if he was deep in thought. Finally, looking up, Nathan saw the eyes of a man who seemed to have lost hope.

"I have not seen you before," the officer said. "You don't wear the uniform of a soldier or militia. Where are you from?"

"Vermont."

"Why are you with us?" he asked.

"I had crossed for personal reasonings but was arrested. They think I am a spy."

"Are you?" he asked.

"No, but no one knows me. There is no way I can prove that I am not." Nathan's voice trailed off.

Each seemed lost in their own thoughts, as the officer continued to twirl the paper with his fingers.

"What is that?" Nathan asked, looking at the paper.

The officer wondered if he should reply or just get up and move elsewhere. Finally, he just shrugged his shoulders.

"It's a letter to my friend, Seneca," he said. "It's about why we lost the battle."

Nathan waited to see if this officer would continue.

"It matters not now. I probably will never see him again and my letter will be lost. Do you want to hear why we lost?" the officer asked. "Let me read it. It may be the last time my story is told."

"Your letter of Sept. 28th this moment I have received, and I can assure you a letter never gave me so much pleasure – a letter from you at any time gives me pleasure, but at this time in particular, just on the eve of a battle, when we know not what our fate will be, to receive a testimony that we have a friend who interests himself in it, and if auspicious, who will drop a tear to our memory is beyond description.

Many whose hardened characters disenable them to claim that he may said, 'what matters it to me whether I am mourned by friends, or not, if death must be my fate!' It is human nature and I cling to it! After what I have written, you will understand that an invasion is to take place – Everything is in preparation for crossing at Queenston to take the enemy's strong place on the hill and then to proceed to Fort George; it is to take place tonight and it is not three o'clock; I have but little time from preparing the men to devote to writing – an attempt was made the night before last – all the Regulars from the Garrison marched up to the Camp at Lewiston with an idea of crossing, but it was defeated in consequence of trusting to a Militia Lieut. To bring a boat loaded with oars to row the other boats across.

A part of the United S. Troops was detached in the morning in order to prepare for crossing, and the rest were marched up after 12 o'clock P.M. – it had been raining during the afternoon, and the roads were very bad and the night very dark, and the rain continued to pour down hard and cold, the Troops suffered – this I witnessed from being placed to bring up the rear, where all that had been sick would fall back when we arrived at Lewiston.

One mile from the camp, we met with fellow soldiers that marched in the morning just marching down to the river to cross – it was intended for them to cross and us to follow and support them.

We built up a fire to warm our soldiers expecting to hear from the party that crossed that day, then to cross immediately; but before that time the unfortunate news came that they could not cross–we immediately returned to the Garrison. If it hadn't been for one man's negligence, it is probable that this would have been written from Canada or not at all."

The officer saw a British soldier moving towards him.

"What is that in your hand?" he ordered.

"Nothing." He tried to hide it in his fist.

"Give it to me now. Or I will give you some of this." He pushed the rifle into the chest of the officer.

The officer released the paper into the hands of the private. Motioning with the rifle, the officer was ordered to follow the private as they made their way to Major Glegg.

Nathan had remained silent, resigned to his fate as a prisoner under British control. With the night descending, the chill in the air prompted the doubling of guards, while the prisoners sought whatever warmth they could find amidst the cool evening air.

By now Mary had entered the gates of Fort George, her steps being purposeful as she halted by the south-east corner. Major Glegg met her near the quarters.

"Miss Johnson?" he asked.

"Yes."

"Thank you for coming. I'll get right to the point. We captured an American two days ago. He has no papers on him, and no officer can vouch for him. He says that he was not with their army. The only thing he can tell us is that he came to Queenston to warn you of the invasion. What can you tell me?"

"If he is who I think he is," she said, "His name is Nathan Douglas. He was a sailor with the schooner Peggy, that brought supplies for Mr. Hamilton's estate last May."

"Then you know him?" the major asked.

"If he is the same man, then yes. Can I see him to make sure?"

"Tell me some more about him."

"His family is from Vermont. I hadn't seen him since May until he came to the estate the night before the invasion. He said that he came to warn me and that I should leave the estate."

"You seem to know quite a bit about him," the major said.

"I barely escaped when the estate was destroyed. He also helped me make sure the Secord family was kept safe while their husband was fighting for you."

"Is he a spy?" the major asked. "Maybe he did these things to throw suspicion off himself. He may really be here to spy for the Americans."

"He is no spy. Just caught in these unfortunate events, as I and many others are. May I see him?"

Major Glegg looked carefully at Mary. If she was lying, her facial expressions would give her away, the twitch of an eyelid, the glance upwards. He saw nothing. Motioning to the private, Nathan was to be brought, but carefully watched. The Major still didn't trust him or any American, regardless of who vouched for him.

Nathan was soon brought to the office of Major Glegg. Seeing Mary, he wanted to move towards her, to pull her close, but the Major was quick to motion him to sit. Mary took the other chair.

"Mary confirms your story. I am not sure that I trust you, but I trust her. She was a friend of General Brock's. He spoke highly of her, and his word was good enough for me. But we still have a problem. You are an American and all Americans must leave Niagara or be imprisoned. Since you are a non-combatant, you will be returned to Fort Niagara. Until these arrangements are made, you are to be kept with the other prisoners. Do you have anything that you want to say?"

"No, sir," Nathan replied.

"Major, may I speak?" Mary had turned towards Nathan. "Would you permit me to have a few moments with Nathan before I leave?"

"You can have five minutes and no more. The private will stay."

The moment seemed awkward, knowing that the private was to report every
word to the Major.

"How is your papa? I heard in Queenston that he is very sick."

"He is better. Mrs. Carter, a neighbor, has been a great help to him and to me. Nathan, what will you do? Will I ever see you again?" She longed to reach out and hold his hand, but not with the private standing there.

"I will make my way back to Vermont, to see how my parents are doing." Nathan knew he needed to choose his words carefully.

"When this war is over, I will find you. I will make my way back to that oak tree and leave you a note."

There are many oak trees in Queenston, but only one that they shared.

"Wrap it up," the private said. "Time to go."

Mary, without being asked, gave Nathan a hug.

"I will wait for you," she whispered in his ear. "I will watch by the tree."

As the private led Nathan back to the compound, Mary resumed her journey homeward. Her steps were lighter now, buoyed by a newfound sense of hope. Deep within her heart, she held onto the belief that somehow, someway, they would find a path back to each other, to be reunited once more.

Reaching home, Mary's spirits soared at the sight of her father sitting upright by the fireplace, surrounded by the comforting presence of Mrs.

Carter and her children. Relief washed over her as she realized that despite the trials they had faced, they were together again, ready to face whatever challenges lay ahead as a family.

"Mary," he said as she came in. "I am so glad to see you."

"Papa." Mary rushed towards him and threw her arms around his neck. "Papa."

His fever had broken. Though still feeling weak, he was so much better than yesterday.

"Papa, Mrs. Carter has been such a great help to us, to me. I could not have done this without her."

Mary reached across to squeeze Mrs. Carter's hand.

"I know," he said, with a twinkle in his eye.

"Papa," Mary laughed. "I don't think I've seen that twinkle for a long time."

Mrs. Carter blushed as she shot a furtive glance towards George.

Stepping back, Mary looked around the home. The beds were made. The kitchen was clean. The broth was boiling. Her papa was better.

"It is going to be okay," she said, "for all of us."

About The Author

David Griggs is a lover of history and especially historical fiction. He had lived in the Niagara Region for many years, where much of this story takes place. Visiting the battles sites, standing in the redan overlooking the Niagara River, gazing upon the shoreline or climbing the stairs to the top of the Brock monument on the heights of Queenston causes the mind to reflect back and appreciate those who fought and died, on both sides of the conflict.

The sequels to "The Coming Storm" have now been published and can be found on Amazon.

"Flames of Faith"

"Whispers of Hope"

Thanks for joining me in this adventure. Happy reading!

Other Books By The Same Author

Hitler's Secret Papers

Crossword Puzzles

Sudoku

Word Searches

Social Media

https://godeeperministries.com